A TASTE of AUSTRALIA

Joy Ross

with assistance from Alistair Punshon

A TASTE of AUSTRALIA

Joy Ross

with assistance from Alistair Punshon

Authentic Australian Cuisine

The Five Mile Press

The Five Mile Press

First published in 1995
by The Five Mile Press Pty. Ltd.
22 Summit Road
Noble Park Victoria 3174 Australia
© Joy Ross

Food styling: Joy Ross and Alistair Punshon
Assistants to food stylists: Kate Maskiell, Georgie O'Shea

With special thanks to Alistair Punshon
for both untiring expertise in his kitchen
and permission to use some of his recipes in this book

Photography: Neil Lorimer

Book design: Geoff Hocking
Cover design: Greg Mason
Editor: Barbara Whiter
Production: Emma Borghesi
Typeset by DigiType, Bendigo, Victoria
Printed by South China Printing Company (1988) Limited

National Library of Australia
Cataloguing-in-Publication data:
Ross, Joy 1942-
A Taste of Australia: authentic Australian cuisine.
ISBN 0 86788 865 2
1. Cookery (Wild foods). 2. Cookery, Australian. I. Title.
641.60994

Acknowledgements:

Kate Punshon and all the staff at the Metropolitan Brasserie and Grill, Bendigo, Victoria
Caroline Long, Cut'n'Dried Flowers, Bendigo
Jo-anne Rogers and the staff of House & Garden, Bendigo
John Perini and the staff of John Perini Tiles, Bendigo
Warehousing Services, Bendigo
Bendigo Pottery, Bendigo
Gabriel Gate Cookware Shop and Cookery Centre, Hawthorn, Victoria

Contents

Introduction

We *are* a lucky country.
The multitude of native fruit, nuts, berries, fish and meat
in Australia, is helping us to create a unique cuisine that reflects
our diversity of culture. The flavours that these healthy foods
provide are tasty and different, and, in the main,
the foods are pesticide-free.

During the 1980s scientists and chefs,
having high regard for the diet of Australia's original inhabitants,
began intense indigenous food research and tastings. Since then,
botanical books which have included some Australian cuisine
recipes have been successfully published.

However, we claim this to be the first elegant,
large format cookbook to showcase the easy-to-prepare and
certainly easy-to-eat, tantalising flavours of uniquely Australian recipes
for the home kitchen. Stunning photography coupled with clear,
methodic recipes will mean your next Australian cuisine dinner
party is talked about for months to come!

The steadily increasing availability in major population
centres throughout Australia of such delights as barramundi and
crabs, bunya bunya nuts, kangaroo and crocodile meats, as well as
indigenous fruits and vegetables, such as quandongs and
Warrigal spinach, has made the creation of this recipe
book a rewarding necessity.

Around the nation, our lands are producing foods
such as emu and kangaroo meat, mainly from Western Australia;
Kakadu plums — which have the world's highest fruit source of
vitamin C — from the Northern Territory, and no-fat bunya bunya
nuts which come from Queensland. Also, Tasmanian salmon has
gained worldwide quality recognition and, in-flight, the Australian
airline Qantas serves Riberry and Illawarra Tart, as well as
offering a variety of indigenous sauces and chutneys.

Within the pages of this book, you will discover
tantalising Australian flavours such as yabby bisque, pan-fried
crocodile nibbles; smoked emu slithers with salad tossed in macadamia
nut oil; buffalo medallions served with asparagus and potato gratin and
the pervasive Aussie kangaroo pie.

You will be delighted and possibly surprised
at just how simple and easy each recipe is to prepare.

For 'chocoholics' and dessert lovers, there's a
delectable Aussie chocolate damper baked in terracotta pots and a
wattle chocolate mousse served with toasted marshmallows.

Winter pudding enthusiasts can try the scrumptious
and crunchy bunya bunya nut pudding. Our great Aussie summer
puddings bulge with Australian muntharies and riberries.

And, we no longer have to borrow the
Devonshire tea from the English! We have created our own
recipe for Aussie tea and wattleseed buns with rosella flower
jam and cream.

Alistair Punshon, who is a partner in the
Metropolitan Brasserie and Grill in Bendigo, Victoria, is an
internationally-renowned chef who assisted in the compilation of
some of the recipes in this book and cooked and tested all the dishes
for photography. He is keen to establish and promote a recognisably
Australian cooking style, and, as a regular guest chef to leading
hotels in Hong Kong and America, is continually researching
and creating new and exciting national dishes.

We hope that these enticingly flavoursome
and healthy recipes will promote a convivial and gastronomic
appreciation of Australian food, both gathered and produced, and
further interest in developing an Australian gastronomic identity —
beginning in the home kitchens of Australia.

The availability of Australian produce is
continually growing and is already sold through speciality food
outlets springing up in major cities and provincial towns. Between
them, they have extensive ranges of fresh produce and packaged goods:
a selection of these suppliers is listed on page 152.

Yes, we certainly are a lucky country...start your Aussie cooking today!

Joy Ross

Melbourne, 1995

SOUP

Soup

We've created some easy soup recipes
which provide entree-size tastings of the diversity of
indigenous ingredients.

Investigate some of these new taste sensations
by creating the popular Kangaroo Tail Soup, or a Mussel
or Oyster Soup. And if you prefer something cold, try the creamy
riesling and native flower combination found in our Chilled
Rosella Flower Soup.

The combining of indigenous nuts in soups
is also a taste treat, particularly the Bunya Bunya Nut Soup with its
Witchetty Grub garnish. The Macadamia and Pear Soup with added
seafood flavours also mingle superbly.

However, remember that the heart of any soup
is its stock. Some, but not all, of our soup recipes require stock.

Fish stock is easy and inexpensive to make.
Just combine fish heads from your local fishmonger, together with
white wine, vegetables and herbs which have been sweated in butter
for a few minutes and simmer for about 25 minutes. Cool and strain.
A good fish stock, when refrigerated, becomes jellied.

Basic ingredients for my vegetable stock
are always carrots, onions, celery, a little garlic and a few bay leaves,
but try varying the herbs depending on your taste and the end use
of the stock. If I have other vegetables available such as
tomatoes and zucchini, they are also added.

To prepare my vegetable stock, I quickly sweat
the finely chopped vegetables before adding the water. To retain the
freshness and flavour, vegetable stock requires only about ten
minutes cooking time. Never use limp vegetables.

Chicken and meat stocks should consist of
fifty percent bones and fifty percent meat. Again, add and sweat
your chosen fresh vegetables, before simmering for about 30 minutes.
White wine is good to add to bone stock, because the acid helps to
release the bones' gelatine. Never boil and always strain a meat stock.

Stocks also freeze well; a bonus for a busy cook.

Cream of Oyster Soup

The eastern coast of Australia, from Tin Can Bay in Queensland and south to Victoria's Mallacoota Inlet, has a prolific supply of rock oysters. Sydney's rock oysters, in particular, have an international reputation for their flavour.

However, not all of us have time to collect rock oysters, so a visit to any Australian fish market is the answer. They always have a plentiful supply of fresh Australian oysters.

24 oysters (retain shells for garnish if desired)
300 ml white wine
1 small carrot, finely diced
2 small shallots, finely chopped
300 ml fish stock
2 egg yolks
80 ml unsweetened cream
50 g butter
garnish (optional) Tasmanian salmon roe or homegrown parsley

Put the oysters in a saucepan and add the wine, carrot and shallots. Pour in the fish stock and simmer for 2 minutes. Remove the oysters. Reduce this stock for 5 minutes.

Blend the egg yolks with the cream and beat into the soup with the butter. Adjust seasonings to taste. Do not boil.

Divide oysters and either leave in shells alongside soup bowls or place them in four hot soup bowls. Pour soup into bowls and garnish.

——— Serves 4 ———

Below: Cream of Oyster Soup

Chilled Rosella Flower Soup

On hot evenings when warm food is not to your liking, try this refreshing summer soup. It's spiked with a little brandy, so it's a bit like a soup aperitif!

This native rosella is not a parrot, but a native hibiscus flower, with a crisp, berry and rhubarb-like taste and a wonderful colour. The flowers can be eaten raw, mixed in salads, poached or used in chutney. (Sour cherries could replace the rosella flowers.)

Thanks go to Alistair Punshon for creating such an impressive combination.

500 g rosella flowers
(see supplier list on page 152)

750 g riesling white wine

cinnamon stick

grated rind of 1 lemon

100 ml brandy

300 ml sour cream

300 ml cream

4 spring onion stems

sprinkled nutmeg

Reserve 8 rosella flowers for garnishing.

Soften remaining flowers by poaching in riesling, to which cinnamon stick and rind has been added. Cool. Puree. Add brandy and chill soup in refrigerator.

When ready to serve, combine the two creams and fold through. Garnish with a dollop of cream, reserved rosella flowers, spring onion stems and a sprinkle of nutmeg.

———— Serves 8 ————

Rosella Flowers

Opposite: Chilled Rosella Flower Soup

Yabby Bisque

A bisque is a rather elegant soup, so you may think that muddy yabbies don't fill the bill. However, the delicate and sweet flavour, together with the firm texture of the wild yabby, is just what this soup requires.

So if you are lucky enough to have wild yabbies, de-muddy them by soaking overnight in salt and water. Change the water in the morning, but keep them soaking until you're ready to cook them. (On the other hand, some people don't mind the muddy flavour.)

To cook yabbies, simply put them into boiling salted water and remove less than a minute after they rise to the surface.

To retain the delicate flavour of the yabbies, the bisque is not swamped with a multitude of ingredients.

16 cooked yabbies
4 cups fish stock
1 cup milk
salt and pepper to taste
¼ teaspoon dry mustard
1 tablespoon butter
1 tablespoon flour
2 eggs
300 ml cream
200 can crushed and peeled tomatoes
2 tablespoons dry sherry
4 yabby claws for garnish

Remove meat from yabbies' tails. Retain four claws and some meat for garnish.

In a large saucepan place fish stock, milk and seasonings. Bring slowly to simmer, but do not boil.

Melt butter in smaller saucepan and stir in flour. Remove from heat and set aside. Take ½ cup of fish liquid and whisk into butter and flour. Whisk eggs and cream together then add to the mixture.

Carefully add mixture to fish stock, add crushed tomatoes and sherry. Simmer for about 5 minutes. Add yabby meat and quickly heat through.

Check the bisque for seasonings, then ladle into preheated bowls. Garnish with yabby claws and meat.

——————— Serves 4 ———————

Opposite: Yabby Bisque

Above: Macadamia and Pear Soup

Macadamia and Pear Soup
—— with Scallops and Prawns ——

Thank goodness for scientist John MacAdam, who studied the nutritional value of the macadamia nut. The nut's fat content is about 70%, but most of this is mono-saturated fat. Macadamia nuts also have a very high energy, protein content.

Like a lot of native food, the less done to it the better. In this recipe we've just roughly chopped the macadamia nuts and quickly cooked the prawns and scallops. They're a great surprise at the end of the meal — it's not often you get to eat such a tasty garnish!

And the just-firm pears provide a little sweetness to the unusual soup combination of nuts, fruit and fish.

125 g roughly chopped macadamia nuts

2 tablespoons oil

2 small, finely chopped onions

3 pears, peeled, and finely sliced into strips

½ teaspoon native thyme
(see supplier list on page 152)

salt
freshly ground pepper

1 cup coconut milk

2 cups water or chicken stock

1 level teaspoon finely chopped red chilli

12 green prawns

12 scallops trimmed with intestine removed

light red chutney (optional)

Saute chopped macadamia nuts in oil until medium brown and place in bowl. Saute onions until translucent. Add pears and saute until soft. Add seasonings, coconut milk, water or stock and chillies, then simmer for 15–20 minutes. When cool, blend the soup and then reheat it to a simmer.

Lightly pan-fry (or barbecue on hot plate) prawns for 2–3 minutes on each side and the scallops for about 1 minute on each side.

Add the macadamia nuts to soup and pour soup into preheated bowls. Garnish with the scallops, prawns and, if desired, a light red chutney. Provide finger bowls.

——————— Serves 4 ———————

Aussie Crayfish Bisque

On the one hand, crayfish soups are exquisitely delicate, yet on the other, enjoyable in the way of peasants living in the Middle Ages, who dunked or mopped-up with bread. Our Pumpkin Seed and Bush Tomato Flatbread (see recipe on page 148) would be a delightful accompaniment.

1 medium, finely chopped onion

1 crushed clove garlic

crushed crayfish body shells

1 tablespoon tomato paste

¼ teaspoon paprika

1 tablespoon butter

1 tablespoon flour

4 cups fish stock

shredded meat from one small cooked crayfish

thin spring onion lengths for garnish

In a heavy-based pan, sweat or saute the onion and garlic. Add crushed crayfish shells, tomato paste and paprika.

In a smaller pan, add butter, melt and then stir in flour. Set aside for one minute and then carefully add 1 cup fish stock.

Add this roux mixture to the ingredients already in the heavy-based pan. Add remaining stock. Over a low heat stir constantly for about 5 minutes, until the bisque has thickened slightly. Do not allow the mixture to boil. Strain well through a food strainer.

Add the shredded crayfish and heat through the strained liquid. Taste, correct seasoning and ladle into preheated bowls. Garnish with thin spring onion lengths.

——————— Serves 2 ———————

Mussel Soup

Sydney might have abundant rock oysters, but Melbourne and Tasmania are known for mussels.

Mussels are such a versatile food, but before preparing them for a meal make sure they are fresh. The shells should be closed; if they are only slightly open, tap them with your finger and if they close straight away, use them. Discard those that don't close.

It's also important to carefully wash the mussel and remove its fibrous, clinging beard.

24 mussels, washed and scrubbed, with beards removed

100 ml dry white wine or water

2 shallots, peeled and chopped

2 tablespoons oil

4 cloves garlic, chopped

60 g butter

60 g flour

4 cups water or light fish stock

1 teaspoon salt

juice of two medium lemons

garnish: parsley or coriander, chopped

Place the prepared mussels into a heavy pan, with wine or water, cover and cook over a gentle heat for 8–10 minutes until mussels open and release their juices.

In another pan, soften the shallots in oil, add the garlic and allow to soften. Melt in the butter, stir in the flour and cook for a few minutes before adding some of the strained mussel juice. When reasonably absorbed, add the water or fish stock, salt and lemon juice. Bring to just below the boil and simmer for 8–10 minutes.

Keep a few mussels in shells for garnish and remove the remainder. Discard any that have not opened during cooking. Warm mussels for just a few minutes. Divide mussels and soup, placing in four, large and warm soup bowls. Sprinkle with the chopped parsley or coriander.

———— Serves 4 ————

Opposite: Mussel Soup

Bunya Bunya Nut Soup
—— with Witchetty Grub Garnish ——

Bunya bunya nuts come from the native bunya pine. During autumn, bunya trees drop huge cones full of seeds. The seeds or nuts are soft, with a similar size and flavour to chestnuts.

Aborigines saw them as an important food source. In fact, scientific studies have shown that the bunya bunya nut has no fat at all. In addition, because of its slow-releasing carbohydrate properties, it's an excellent food for diabetics.

However, if you can't collect bunya bunya nuts in autumn, then you can keep a supply of these nuts in your freezer — see supplier list on page 152. Pecan nuts could be substituted (they are grown in Australia), but the purpose of this book is to try our native produce, not introduced crops.

When roasted, so that it has crispy skin and soft flesh, a witchetty grub is another taste thriller. The grub is actually a wood-boring, edible caterpillar of an Australian moth. However, the easiest way to taste witchetty grubs, is to buy them in a can (again see supplier list) and use the grub as a garnish. Be adventurous! My husband says that if he were offered a tray of hors d'oeuvres, he would choose a seared witchetty grub first every time.

2¼ litres chicken stock
2 sticks celery, chopped
3 small leeks, sliced
20 boiled and peeled bunya bunya nuts (see supplier list on page 152)
½ butternut pumpkin, peeled
4 bay leaves
salt
freshly ground pepper
300 ml cream
1 teaspoon butter
1 can witchetty grubs (see supplier list on page 152)

In a large saucepan, bring chicken stock to the boil and add celery and leeks. Roughly chop bunya bunya nuts and pumpkin and add to the now simmering stock. Add bay leaves, salt and ground pepper and simmer for 1–1¼ hours.

Cool the soup and puree. Blend in two-thirds of the cream. When ready to serve, place butter in a hot pan and quickly sear/panfry eight witchetty grubs. This will take only 1–2 minutes.

Heat soup and pour into preheated plates. Float a dollop of cream in centre of each soup bowl and place a witchetty grub on top of the cream.

—————— Serves 4 ——————

Opposite: Bunya Bunya Nut Soup

Kangaroo Tail Soup
—— with Wattleseed Linguini ——

Interstate and overseas visitors know of and are keen to taste kangaroo tail soup. Unique to Australia, the kangaroo has one of the lowest cholesterol levels of all the red meats.

If made the day before, the soup will have had time for the flavours to mature. Whenever you choose to prepare it, cooking takes about three and a half to four hours, so there's plenty of time to enjoy yourself between the preparing and eventual sipping of this fine soup. And it's well worth the effort.

If the split peas are cooked for the entire time, then there isn't any need to soak them overnight. On the other hand, I always find that lentils have a much softer consistency if overnight soaking has taken place — I'll leave it to you!

Kangaroo tails are available at some supermarkets, as well as at produce markets and delicatessans throughout Australia.

8 joints of kangaroo tail   (see supplier list on page 152)
plain flour
60 g butter
1 cup split peas, soaking is optional
2 litres meat or vegetable stock
1 teaspoon salt
2 diced, medium carrots
1 small, peeled and diced turnip
2 onions, sliced
2 chopped cloves garlic
1 dessertspoon brown sugar
2 bay leaves
2 pinches dry native thyme   (see supplier list on page 152)
salt
freshly ground pepper
wattleseed linguini   (see supplier list on page 152)
ground bush tomato   (see supplier list on page 152)

Dust kangaroo tail with a little flour. Melt half the butter in a pan, add the kangaroo joints and cook until they're brown on the outside. Remove and place in a large saucepan.

Add split peas, cover with stock and salt. Bring to the boil slowly, skimming the top occasionally. Cover and cook gently for about 2½ hours.

Melt the additional butter and, very lightly, saute vegetables. When the joint has been cooking for about two hours, add sauteed vegetables, brown sugar, bay leaves and thyme. Add additional salt and pepper to taste. Simmer for another hour. Check and stir periodically.

When cool enough to handle, remove kangaroo tail with slotted spoon, and if preferred, slice the meat from bone, discarding any fatty or hard sections.

Return meat to soup and chill so that any fat can easily be removed from the top. When required reheat.

Cook enough linguini according to directions for 4 small garnishing serves. Serve soup in preheated bowls and sprinkle with ground bush tomato. Garnish with wattleseed linguini.

—————— Serves 4 ——————

Above: Kangaroo Tail Soup

Sweet Potato Soup

Sweet potato tubers grow in tropical and semi-tropical regions. There is a white-fleshed sweet potato, but I always use the orange-fleshed variety, because there is less discolouration in cooking and its colour is spectacular.

The soup of the sweet potato is delicious whether served hot or chilled.

The traditional way to soften these large tubers is to wash and bake them in the oven for one to one and a half hours. However, by running a large tuber under the tap and then placing it in a microwave on high, the sweet potato is cooked in about 25 minutes.

350 g sweet potato
4 cups chicken stock
1 cup cream
1 level teaspoon curry powder
1 teaspoon salt
¼ teaspoon freshly ground pepper
garnish: grated nutmeg

Remove the potato from the oven or microwave, cool, slit down the middle and spoon the softened flesh into a food processor. Gradually add chicken stock and blend until a puree consistency. Blend in cream, curry powder, salt and ground pepper.

Heat through on low heat. Serve in warm bowls and garnish with grated nutmeg.

——— Serves 4–6 ———

ENTREES

Entrees

Much of the pleasure of eating
is the joy of surrounding yourself with friends and discussing
new taste sensations.

Australian native food is no exception.
In fact, its popularity now is not just attributed to a few
dishes at leading Australian restaurants. Throughout Australia
there are many suburban hotels and bistros serving meals such as
crocodile in risotto, kangaroo steaks and wallaby hamburgers.
There are also a number of restaurants
serving only native food.

This chapter enables you to try some
of these delicious flavours in small serves. You'll certainly create
a lot of comment if you serve a plate of indigenous food
with drinks before a meal.

Smoked emu slithers with a smidgen
of bush tomato sauce on small, buttered pumpkin scones are a
real hit. Pan-fried crocodile and herb nibbles with Kakadu plums
and homemade cured salmon slices are certainly
sought-after treats.

While marron gourmet bites or
the wattleseed in our prawn crepes are not everyday foods,
do look for the numerous recipes using Australia's famous
and more accessible macadamia nuts to add interest to
any lunch or dinner party.

Next time you have a party,
create a mix of native foods and see the reaction. The visual impact
of this food is appetizingly elegant, enticing and very special.
I think you'll find there will be
a lot of conversation!

Avocado and Macadamia Nut Cheese Mound

Macadamia nuts were Australia's first commercially grown native food. Both aborigines and early settlers saw the nut as an excellent food source.

Like a lot of native food, the less done to it the better. Macadamia nuts are delightful when eaten raw, or simply roasted and added to this avocado and cheese recipe.

½ ripe avocado
1 tablespoon mild mustard
250 g Australian cream cheese
150 g roasted macadamia pieces
ground pepper
chopped coriander/parsley to coat
75 g whole roasted macadamia nuts
water biscuits or toasted bread triangles

Remove the avocado flesh and mash. Add mustard.

Blend the cream cheese until smooth.

Swirl the avocado mix through the cream cheese. Add 100 g macadamia pieces.

Form a mound, roll in ground pepper and coriander or parsley mix.

Place on a serving plate, surrounding base with whole macadamias and sprinkle with remaining macadamia pieces.

Serve with water biscuits or toasted triangles with before-dinner drinks or as an appetizer for 4.

——— Serves 4 ———

Below: Avocado and Macadamia Nut Cheese Mound

Marron Gourmet Bites
—— served with Lemon Myrtle Mayonnaise ——

Marrons are an Australian freshwater crayfish, often regarded as the sweetest and finest of the crayfish meats. In Western Australia and Queensland they are farmed for national and international gourmet eating.

Many marron enthusiasts place freshly caught marrons in their freezers just long enough to stun the fish, but not long enough to freeze the flesh. If plunged live into boiling water, the flesh can be tough. Over-cooking of any crayfish is a crime.

Lemon myrtle is a rainforest tree farmed on the east coast of Australia. The leaves have a refreshing flavour similar to a blend of lemon, lime and lemongrass.

2 marrons (dependent on size, but enough for 4 people)

white wine

native peppercorns
(see supplier list on page 152)

salt

mild mayonnaise

1 bottle of lemon myrtle oil
(see supplier list on page 152)

Take marrons from freezer. Add wine and seasonings to boiling water, drop in marrons and remove less than a minute after they rise to the surface. At this stage they will have bright red shells.

Dunk marrons in cold water. When coolish, twist the head from the edible tail and take out the meat.

Add a few drops of lemon myrtle oil to a plain mayonnaise and serve with marron morsels.

—— Serves 4 ——

Pan-fried Crocodile Nibbles
—— served with Kakadu Plums ——

Crocodile meat is delicious, white and quite filling. It has a similar colour and flavour to a cross between pork and chicken. Its flesh is fairly watery and fibrous, but not tough.

In looks a Kakadu plum is slightly more elongated than a green olive. It is found within the Kakadu area of the Northern Territory (not the national park) across to the Kimberley region of Western Australia. It has a rather delicate, mild-apricot flavour and it is the world's highest fruit source of vitamin C.

400 g crocodile meat (approximately)
(see supplier list on page 152)

olive oil

fresh herbs — dill, coriander and parsley

4 tablespoons white wine

1 packet frozen Kakadu plums
(see supplier list on page 152)

2 tablespoons butter

1 finely chopped clove garlic

Below: Pan-fried Crocodile Nibbles

For maximum flavour, marinate the meat overnight in oil, half the herbs and white wine.

Thaw Kakadu plums.

Melt butter, add garlic and, on medium heat, add the marinated crocodile meat, and saute for a few minutes. It's important not to overcook the meat. Add remaining herbs and toss through.

Serve as nibbles, or as an appetizer for 4 serves. Garnish with Kakadu plums.

Crayfish Mousse Tuckerbag
—— with Spring Onion Tie and Ginger Dipping Sauce ——

In Australia, the names crayfish and lobster are both used to describe the sea crayfish caught in Australian waters. The freshwater species of crayfish include marron, yabbies and Murray River crayfish.

The easiest way to make this mousse is to buy a cooked crayfish and remove the meat. If the crayfish is small, add some finely cut crab meat to ensure the meat quantity is met.

1 packet of 12 fillo pastry sheets
butter
spring onions for tying
500 g cooked crayfish meat (or mix crayfish and crab meat)
1 tablespoon native lime juice (see supplier list on page 152)
salt and pepper to taste
¾ cup cream
3 stiffly beaten egg whites
Herman's Ginger Dipping Sauce (see supplier list on page 152, or our recipe below)

Preheat oven to 180°C.

Thaw fillo pastry and using four sheets per tuckerbag, butter sheets according to the manufacturer's instructions. Blanch about 8 long spring onions.

In a food processor, place crayfish (or crayfish and crab) meat, lime juice and salt and pepper. Process until meat is finely chopped. Add cream and mix well. Remove from food processor into a bowl and fold through egg whites. Cool.

Place all four fillo pastry preparations on bench. Divide fish mixture and place equal proportions in the centre of each pastry base. With both hands, bunch up all the pastry points to the centre of the mousse and tie with spring onions. Place in preheated oven for 30–40 minutes.

Serve with ginger dipping sauce.

———— Serves 4 ————

Ginger Dipping Sauce

125 g sugar
250 ml water
4 lemon myrtle leaves (see supplier list on page 152)
125 ml white wine vinegar
red chilli sauce
40 g ginger root, peeled and grated
sliced red chillies
sliced shallots

Put sugar, water and lemon myrtle leaves into a saucepan and heat gently, stirring constantly until sugar is dissolved. Bring to the boil and boil for 2 minutes. Cool, leaving lemon myrtle leaves in sugar syrup.

When cool, add white wine vinegar, red chilli sauce and grated ginger root.

Garnish with sliced red chilli and sliced shallots.

———— Makes about 500 ml ————

Opposite: Crayfish Mousse Tuckerbag

Emu Slithers on Pumpkin Scones
—— with Bush Tomato Sauce ——

Emu meat was the first game meat to be farmed in Australia and has a similar taste to, but is not as strong as, venison. On the other hand, pumpkin scones are synonymous with an ex-Queensland Premier's wife, retired Senator Flo Bjelke-Petersen, who loved to serve them to her guests. Her recipe was freely given to those who wanted to make this popular savoury.

By adding the native bush tomato's distinct flavour, the combination of emu, pumpkin and bush tomato is certainly a new Australian taste sensation.

40 g butter
¼ cup caster sugar
1 lightly beaten egg
¾ cup cooked pumpkin
2½ cups self-raising flour
½ teaspoon ground nutmeg
⅓ cup milk, approximately
1 small smoked emu leg   *(see supplier list on page 152)*
butter to spread on scones — optional
bush tomato sauce   *(see supplier list on page 152)*
parsley or coriander garnish

Preheat oven to 250°C. Lightly grease 2 × 20 cm round sandwich pans or cake tins.

Beat butter and sugar in a small bowl with an electric mixer until light and fluffy. Gradually beat in egg and transfer to a large bowl.

Stir in pumpkin, then sifted flour and nutmeg and enough milk to make a soft, sticky dough. Turn dough onto lightly floured surface and knead lightly until smooth. Press dough out to about 2 cm in thickness and cut 5 cm rounds from dough.

Place scones, just touching, in prepared pans. Brush with a little milk. Bake in a very hot oven for about 12–15 minutes.

Makes about 16.

Meanwhile, slice small, fine slithers of emu to fit on top of cut scones.

When scones are cooked, slightly cool them before cutting in half and spreading with butter and/or bush tomato sauce.

Top with slithers of emu.

—————— Serves 6 ——————

Opposite: Emu Slithers on Pumpkin Scones

Crumbed Oysters and Fried Parsley
—— with Illawarra Plum and Chilli Sauce ——

Raw oysters, dribbled with lemon juice and ground pepper and served in a half shell, have worldwide popularity. In fact, some oyster lovers won't eat them any other way.

However, a complete change of pace is to try them lightly crumbed and quickly pan-fried.

½ cup plain flour with pinch salt and sprinkle pepper
1 lightly beaten egg
1 cup fine breadcrumbs
24 fresh oysters
1 tablespoon olive oil
1 tablespoon butter
paper towel
1 teaspoon oil
1 teaspoon butter
½ bunch washed and dried parsley, complete with stalks
Illawarra Plum and Chilli Sauce (see recipe on page 40)

Place seasoned flour, egg and breadcrumbs — one item in each of three bowls.

Flour, egg and breadcrumb each oyster.

Heat oil and butter in large pan and, for about a minute, on one side quickly fry half the breadcrumbed oysters. Turn and remove after half a minute. Place cooked oysters on paper towel and keep warm. Add uncooked oysters to the pan and repeat the above steps.

Heat oil and butter for parsley. Quickly fry parsley over high heat.

Serve 6 crumbed oysters on each plate, garnish with parsley and Illawarra Plum and Chilli Sauce — see separate recipe for this sauce on page 40.

—— Serves 4 ——

Prawn and Avocado Baby Wattleseed Crepes
—— with Illawarra Plum and Chilli Sauce ——

Most prawns are found in the warmer, northern waters of Australia.

Like most crustaceans the simplest cooking preparation usually ends up with the best results. The prawn flavour is so delicate that any heavy ingredients served with them tend to be too dominant.

Because of their soft and very tasty flesh, avocados are a great accompaniment for prawns. They are usually sold green and will take a couple of days to ripen.

Wattleseed is a blended mix of several species of Australian wattle and, following the macadamia nut, is the second commercialised native plant species on the market. After being steeped in water, wattleseed grounds can be used in an endless array of savoury and sweet dishes.

2 teaspoons of wattleseed (see supplier list on page 152)	1 garlic clove, crushed
1 cup plain flour	½ cup bush tomato chutney (see supplier list on page 152)
enough milk to make mixture runny	1 soft and ripe avocado, mashed
4 stiffly beaten egg whites	300 g peeled, chopped and cooked prawns
pinch salt	75 ml cream
1 tablespoon butter	1 firm avocado for slicing
1 small onion, sliced	Illawarra Plum and Chilli Sauce (see recipe on page 40)
½ capsicum, sliced	

Crepe: To soften the wattleseed grounds, bring two teaspoons of wattleseed and ½ cup of water to the boil. Strain liquid. Blend flour, milk, beaten egg whites and salt together, add the drained wattleseed and set aside.

Prawn sauce: Melt butter and cook onion, capsicum and garlic until tender. Stir in bush tomato chutney and mashed avocado. Remove tract that runs down the back of the prawn tail. Add prawns and cream. Set aside.

Lightly grease a pan with butter before making at least 12 baby crepes. Stack cooked crepes in a pile, with a sheet of grease-proof paper separating each one.

Re-heat the prawn sauce.

Spoon prawn sauce mixture into cooled crepes, garnish with avocado slices and serve with sauce.

——————— Serves 4 ———————

Blue Swimmer Crabs
—— with Onions in Beer ——

The stunningly coloured blue swimmer crabs are usually caught in cone-shaped traps. Once trapped or netted, they require soaking.

If your crabs are not alive, keep them in the coldest part of your refrigerator. When you cook them, they change from that wonderful blue to bright orange.

salt and water
1 tablespoon butter
1 teaspoon oil
8 medium, finely sliced onions
⅓ can of 375 ml beer
4 very fresh blue swimmer crabs

In a large pot, bring salted water to the boil. While the water is boiling, heat butter and oil in a heavy-based pan. Sweat onions and then add approximately ⅓ can beer and cook through. Drink the remaining beer!

Meanwhile, add blue swimmers to boiling water. They will instantly change colour and come to the surface. Cook for just a few minutes, being careful not to over-cook.

Place some onions in the translucent beer sauce and a blue swimmer crab on each plate.

——————— Serves 4 ———————

Above: Blue Swimmer Crabs

Moreton Bay Bugs
—— in Champagne Cream Sauce ——

The delicious and popular Moreton Bay bugs are found in the waters off the coast of Queensland. Further south are the Balmain bugs which are broader around the head than the Moreton Bay bugs.

The champagne cream sauce is easy to make and adds a little sweetness to the bugs.

This light meal can be extremely quick if you buy bug meat or bugs already cooked. Simply make a champagne sauce and serve. Although the stock can be made from a stock cube, it's more delectable if it's homemade with fish bones. (See soup chapter introduction for further discussion about stocks).

40 ml champagne
40 ml fish stock
80 ml thickened cream
2 tablespoons white wine
dash of cognac
2 tablespoons unsweetened whipped cream
salt
freshly ground pepper
12 uncooked Moreton Bay bugs

Pour the champagne and fish stock into a pan and reduce by half. Add the cream, white wine and cognac and reduce until sauce thickens.

Carefully fold in whipped cream and season to taste.

The bugs, like most crustaceans, are best kept alive until cooked. The best method is to stun them by placing bugs in the freezer, but not long enough to freeze the flesh.

When ready to cook, place bugs in boiling water. When they rise to the top, give them about half a minute then remove with slotted spoon. Dunk bugs in cold water.

Break tails carefully away from body. With scissors, snip down centre of soft shell on underside, pull apart and gently ease out the soft tail meat.

Discard heads and most of the shells.

Serve with the champagne sauce and garnish with a few pieces of shell.

——— Serves 4–6 ———

Opposite: Moreton Bay Bugs

Marinated Scallops in Warrigal Spinach Parcels
—— served with a Mango Coulis ——

Scallops are, like all shellfish, at their best when very fresh. Sometimes you can buy scallops which have been swollen by being soaked in water to give the illusion of being larger. However, the water is lost in the cooking and the scallops become tougher. So always insist on dry-shucked scallops.

24 dry-shucked scallops, with membranes and intestines removed

30 g chopped pickled ginger

200 g Warrigal spinach
(see supplier list on page 152)

2 peeled, seeded and roughly chopped mangoes

1 tablespoon sour cream

5 tablespoons dry white wine

freshly ground pepper

salt

Marinate the scallops with ginger for 20–25 minutes.

Blanch the Warrigal spinach for a few minutes, drain and refresh in iced water.

Puree the mangoes and sour cream together until smooth.

When marinating scallops are ready, poach scallops and ginger in white wine and seasonings for 1 minute. Drain and cool.

Wrap scallops in pieces of spinach. Quickly heat mango coulis and spread on 4 plates. Arrange 6 scallop parcels on each plate.

——— Serves 4 ———

Illawarra Plum and Chilli Sauce

The Illawarra plum is purple/brown in colour with an external seed. The edible area is the larger, swollen stem. It grows well in the rainforests along Australia's eastern coast and can be used in sauces, jams and tarts. The fruit is slightly bitter and should not be tasted when hot: the bitterness lessens when cool.

Alistair Punshon derived this sauce which complements a whole host of food; the fruit and vegetable combination of plum and chilli, adds that special spark to hot or cold dishes.

200 g Illawarra plums
(see supplier list on page 152)

150 ml water

100 ml port

80 ml brown sugar

70g red currant jelly

15 g chilli sauce

20 ml vinegar

squeeze of lemon juice

salt and pepper

Poach plums in the water, port and brown sugar and when cooked, puree them.

Add all the other ingredients, except seasonings, and simmer until soft and thick. Season with pepper and salt to taste.

Ladle into sterilised jars, seal and store.

——— Makes about 500 ml ———

Opposite: Marinated Scallops in Warrigal Spinach Parcels

Yabby Timbale Pate

There are several species of freshwater crayfish in Australia and the yabby is one of them. It has the shape of a lobster, but only the size of a king prawn. Its one enormous claw is larger on the male of the species.

If these native crustaceans are caught in muddy streams or dams, they need to be soaked overnight and kept alive until they are cooked.

Salt must be added to the water that yabbies are boiled in and a few fresh herbs like dill, can also be added. For this recipe, yabbies should not be boiled for more than three minutes. When cooked, drain and allow to cool.

1 kg cooked yabbies
2 eggs
90 ml cream
freshly ground pepper
salt to taste

Twist the head off and remove yabby meat from tail.

Place all the yabby meat and the eggs into a food processor. With the processor still running, gradually add the cream.

Remove the mixture from processor and add salt and ground pepper.

To make the timbales, divide the mixture evenly into 4 buttered dariole or half-cup moulds. Bake at 180°C for about 15 minutes until risen and slightly set.

Leave timbales to stand for about 2 minutes before turning them out onto warmed plates. Serve with your favourite water cracker biscuits and pumpernickel rounds, garnishing with yabby shells.

————— Serves 4 —————

Opposite: Yabby Timbale Pate

Cured Salmon or Trout

With hors d'oeuvres it's great to serve a variety of interesting food.
Today people tend to eat lightly, but really like to taste and appreciate all the
different flavours. They certainly can do this with cured salmon or trout and its
various accompaniments.

Alistair Punshon kindly told me how he makes this relatively simple,
yet very impressive presentation.

500 g sugar
250 g salt
chopped parsley
chopped dill
4 ground lemon myrtle leaves (see supplier list on page 152)
500 g salmon or trout
100 ml white wine

Combine sugar and salt and place half of the mixture on a large plastic or stainless steel tray.

Combine parsley, dill and ground lemon myrtle leaves and sprinkle half over salt and sugar.

Place fish on mixtures and then top with remaining mixture. Sprinkle with white wine.

Leave the fish to cure for about 12 to 18 hours. The curing time is dependent on thickness of fish and how cured you like your fish. The tail will take less time to cure. But the longer the fish cures the more transparent and chewier it becomes.

When your cured salmon or trout is ready for the table, serve in slithers with any of the following accompaniments — dill sour cream, apple and horseradish salsa, grated Granny Smith apple, or freshly grated horseradish — salt and black ground pepper.

——— Serves 6–8 ———

Lemon Myrtle Leaves

Above: Cured Salmon or Trout

FISH

Fish

Australia has a multitude of fish, crustaceans
and molluscs. We're so lucky to have this wide choice of
fresh fish, because fish is so adaptable and versatile in our diet.

We also often forget just how quick
and easy it is to prepare: substantial and elegant meals can be
presented on the table in less than fifteen minutes.

Our chapter offers recipes from across
the whole continent: from Top End barramundi through to
southern Tasmanian salmon and King Island crayfish. From the
east coast to the west there are mud crabs and Western
Australian marrons.

In between, we have further exciting
recipes including Eucalyptus Skewered Prawns and
Baked Mullet in Banana Leaves.

These tempting recipes are prepared
in a variety of ways — baked, braised, steamed, poached, grilled
or sauteed. They are all relatively simple dishes where, to be
creatively native, we've blended the familiar with some
of the less known.

If a particular fish is not available
when you want to use a recipe, just ask your fishmonger
about an alternative Australian variety. In the markets that I frequent,
fishmongers are eager to help not just with an alternative fish,
but with verbal recipes on how to cook them. Again,
they're usually simple recipes and that's the best way
to obtain maximum flavour from fish.

Remember that any extra ingredients
should be light in consistency and flavour, and fish should never
be overcooked.

Fish market stallholders are always willing
to prepare the fish to your liking, so I always use their services.

Fish's greatest bonus for me is,
because of its protein content, when I buy fresh Australian fish,
I psychologically *feel* healthier — and I probably am!

Curried Tasmanian Scallops
—— with Cooked Pineapple ——

Scallops are so easy to prepare for the table. They are an extremely versatile shellfish that can be poached, fried, barbecued or used in souffles, creamy sauces and salads. For top quality scallops always ask for dry-shucked scallops.

In this quick and tasty recipe the pineapple's sweetness balances beautifully with the dash of coconut milk and curried scallops.

2 × 1.5 cm thick slices pineapple
2 teaspoons mild curry powder
a few freshly chopped herbs
2 teaspoons butter
250 g dry-shucked scallops, remove membranes and intestines
1–2 tablespoons coconut milk
chopped coriander or parsley

Cut pineapple into thin and small finger-size pieces. Grill until slightly brown on both sides. Place on plate and keep warm.

Heat a heavy-based pan and, with the pan dry, quickly brown curry powder and herbs.

Add butter to the curry and herb mix and gently toss-fry scallops for about 1 minute.

Drizzle coconut milk on top of scallops and heat through.

Place scallops and pineapple on preheated plates and garnish with coriander or parsley.

———— Serves 2 ————

Country Breakfast Trout
—— with Peppered and Ground Bush Tomato ——

Although an introduced species, today trout is commonplace around Australia.

The popular rainbow and brown trout are prolific in Australia's cooler, southern waters and ocean trout is now being successfully farmed in Tasmania.

Coral trout are widely dispersed around the coral reef waters of Queensland, the Northern Territory and Western Australia. Equally, if you wake up early and are camped by a mountain stream, trout makes a wonderful pan-fried breakfast. Alternatively, you can buy some trout, dream of free-flowing streams and cook it in your own kitchen.

It's important not to over-cook trout, because the delicate flavour will be lost and the fish will be too dry to really enjoy.

Wild limes can be found in Australia's rainforest and arid areas — see supplier list on page 152. They have a strong, tart lime flavour and a yellow/green skin.

Ground bush tomato and pepper provide a final flavoursome touch.

2 large trout
1 squeezed native lime   *(see supplier list on page 152)*
½ cup seasoned flour
1 tablespoon butter
1 teaspoon oil
ground bush tomato   *(see supplier list on page 152)*
ground pepper
1 native lime cut into wedges   *(see supplier list on page 152)*

Have your fishmonger prepare the fish, or gut, scale and rinse the trout yourself.

Wipe fish with lime juice and coat in seasoned flour. Warm pan, add butter, oil and when sizzling, add floured fish.

Cook for a couple of minutes on both sides. Turn very carefully until you have golden brown trout. Add some pepper to your ground bush tomato, sprinkle over trout and serve immediately with native lime wedges.

—————— Serves 2 ——————

Opposite: Country Breakfast Trout

Baked Barramundi Fillets and Lemon Aspen
—— in Paperbark with a Compote of Tomato and Onion ——

Also known as giant perch, barramundi is a very popular fish of both fishermen and food lovers. Aboriginals often wrapped this sweet and firm, white fleshed fish in ginger leaves.

Today paperbark (see supplier list on page 152), is the preferred wrapping. If you place a few drops of lemon aspen oil on each piece of uncooked bark, when the fish is cooked and the bark opened, the aroma is magic.

The tomato and onion compote provides a good balance to the magic.

50 g butter
4 medium, finely sliced onions
40 ml red wine
4 medium, roughly chopped tomatoes
1 level teaspoon dried basil
2 teaspoons Worcestershire sauce
1 teaspoon brown sugar
½ teaspoon salt
2 barramundi fish fillets
olive oil
2 sprigs of rosemary
lemon aspen oil (see supplier list on page 152)
2 paperbark wrappers (see supplier list on page 152)
twine/string/cotton
freshly ground pepper
chopped parsley

In a shallow pan, sweat the onions in the butter, add the red wine, tomatoes, basil, Worcestershire sauce, brown sugar and salt. Cover and cook for a further 10 minutes before placing in greased compote. Cover.

Prepare fish by rubbing barramundi with oil and placing a piece of rosemary on each. Sprinkle a few drops of lemon aspen oil on the paperbark, wrap fish and tie. Sit parcels on oven tray.

Place the fish and the tomato and onion compote separately in a preheated 180°C oven for about 20 minutes.

On large, preheated plates, serve the barramundi placed on the tomato and onion. Sprinkle with freshly ground pepper and garnish with chopped parsley.

By the way, for an interesting touch, serve the dish in the bark to the table — looks impressive!

—— Serves 2 ——

Crab and Avocado Fish Pie
—— topped with Tasmanian Salmon Roe ——

This is a very attractive cold meal which can be served alone or with smoked salmon, carpaccio of beef or with tomato and goat's cheese slices.

Crab meat and avocados are wholesome foods, both of which are relatively inexpensive. For mashing ease, avocados need to be soft.

Opposite: Baked Barramundi Fillets and Lemon Aspen

3 sheets ready-rolled puff pastry

1 egg yolk

2 large and soft avocados

75 g finely chopped crab meat

1 finely chopped, round shallot

2 tablespoons lime juice

salt

freshly ground pepper

a sprinkling of chilli powder

garnish with 1 or 2 × 50 g jars of large salmon roe

Preheat oven to 200°C.

Cut a large fish shape from one sheet of puff pastry. Cut 4 × 1½ cm wide strips from each remaining pastry sheet and, using two strips, cover both outside edges of shape. With pastry brush, egg yolk the outside strip and lay the other two strips on top of the first strip. Prick all of the pastry and brush with the remaining egg yolk.

Bake for 10–15 minutes until golden brown. The centre will puff up so halfway through cooking, press it down so that it's lower than the border.

Remove from oven, cool.

Mash 2 avocados, stir in crab meat, shallots, lime juice and sprinkle with seasonings.

Fill cooked pastry shell with the avocado and crab mixture. Garnish lightly or thickly with large salmon roe, according to your taste.

——————— Serves 6–8 ———————

Below: Crab and Avocado Fish Pie

Grilled Eucalyptus Skewered Prawns
—— on a Potage of Queensland Pumpkin garnished with Snow Peas ——

Queensland pumpkin might have a hard skin, but its cooked flesh is delicious. It also provides substance for the delicate prawns and stir-fried snow peas. And the eucalyptus butter not only enhances the flavour, but adds a delightful aroma.

Please note that eucalyptus or gum leaf oil is a special food preparation. Do not use normal household eucalyptus or fragrant eucalyptus oils.

1 kg chopped Queensland pumpkin	*8 metal skewers* *(If wooden skewers are used, soak in cold water for 30 minutes or so to stop them charring when used under the grill.)*
1 finely chopped onion	
1 finely chopped and cored apple	
1 cup vegetable or chicken stock	*the juice of 2 native limes* *(see supplier list on page 152)*
½ teaspoon nutmeg	
salt	*a quantity of eucalyptus herb butter* *(see recipe on page 103)*
½ cup water	
½ cup milk	*1 teaspoon butter*
1 kg green king prawns	*1 teaspoon oil*
8 bacon slices cut into small pieces	*sufficient snow peas to serve 4*
	freshly ground pepper

Below: Grilled Eucalyptus Skewered Prawns

Place chopped pumpkin, onion, apple, stock, nutmeg and salt in heavy-based saucepan with the water and milk, and bring to the boil.

Cover and simmer for about 30 minutes until pumpkin is tender.

Drain any excess liquid and mash or puree pumpkin potage. Keep warm.

Peel and de-vein prawns, leaving tails on. Thread prawns and bacon pieces alternately onto skewers, and rub prawns with lime juice.

Place the filled skewers on a grill plate and cook for 2–3 minutes on each side. Baste with eucalyptus butter.

While prawns are grilling, heat a little butter and oil in pan and gently stir fry snow peas for 1–2 minutes.

Divide pumpkin potage between four preheated plates and sprinkle with pepper. Place 2 prawn skewers on each plate of pumpkin and garnish with snow peas.

——————— Serves 4 ———————

Mud Crabs with Tropical Fruit

In Australia, crabs are plentiful and an excellent food source. Mud crabs are usually considered the most delicious of all the crab meats. They're caught either in wire netting cages called crab pots, or in netting bags filled with bait.

8 wooden skewers
½ pineapple
¼ watermelon
½ honeydew melon
½ paw paw
2 mangoes
1 tablespoon brandy — optional
2 tablespoons native lime juice   *(see supplier list on page 152)*
4 cooked mud crabs
2 tablespoons oil
4 drops lemon myrtle oil   *(see supplier list on page 152)*
2 finely chopped cloves garlic
2 teaspoon grated fresh ginger
½ cup finely chopped macadamia nuts

Prepare sufficient fruit to fill 8 skewers.

With variations in colour, thread fruit attractively. Mix brandy and lime juice and brush fruit with the mix.

Cut crabs in half, using meat mallet or nut cracker.

Heat both oils in a wok and stir-fry garlic, ginger and nuts. Add crabs to wok and heat through with the stir-fried ingredients.

Serve crab halves equally onto 4 plates and place two tropical fruit skewers alongside each crab serving.

——————— Serves 4 ———————

Opposite: Mud Crabs with Tropical Fruit

King Island Crayfish
—— with King Island Tasty Cheese Mornay ——

King Island might only be a tiny land mass in Bass Strait where the winds can howl and the seas roar, but because of this clean, bracing climate, its dairy products, crayfish and game are first class.

Not only mainlanders, but international tourists and leading chefs, know of the excellence of King Island products. But unless you're privileged enough to visit the island, your only alternative is to buy their products on the mainland.

1 medium cooked crayfish
15 g butter
½ small, chopped onion
1 tablespoon flour
⅓ cup milk
1 tablespoon dry white wine
1 heaped tablespoon grated King Island Tasty cheese
½ tablespoon French mustard
½ tablespoon English mustard
breadcrumbs
dobs of butter

Halve the crayfish lengthwise and remove meat. Cut into chunks.

Melt butter and saute onion until tender. Add the flour and stir over a low heat for 1 minute. Gradually add the milk and allow the sauce to thicken. Add the wine and simmer for 1 minute, before stirring in cheese and mustards.

Spoon a little of the sauce into the crayfish shells, add the crayfish meat and coat with the remaining sauce. Sprinkle with breadcrumbs and dot with butter. Grill until brown and bubbling. Eat immediately.

—— Serves 2 ——

Poached Rainbow Trout

with Paprika Sauce and Avocado garnished with
—— Lemon Myrtle Vinaigrette ——

This is an easy recipe where the rainbow trout is simply poached and, instead of using the normal avocado vinaigrette, we're introducing lemon myrtle. Poaching temperature should be well below boiling and liquid should just cover the fish.

2 avocados

lemon myrtle vinaigrette
(see supplier list on page 152)

2 tablespoons white wine

1 cup water

2 rainbow trout fillets

1 tablespoon butter

1 tablespoon oil

½ teaspoon paprika

freshly ground native pepper
(see supplier list on page 152)

Peel and halve avocados. Carefully cut halves into slithers and sprinkle with lemon myrtle vinaigrette. Set aside.

Using a heavy-based pan add wine and water and bring to boil. Reduce to a poaching temperature and place fish in gently simmering water and cook for about 3 minutes or just until flesh turns white. Turn once and be careful not to overcook.

Meanwhile, melt butter and oil in second pan and stir through paprika.

Carefully remove trout fillets from liquid and serve rainbow trout on preheated plates. Top with paprika sauce. Garnish with avocado slices and a little more lemon myrtle vinaigrette. Sprinkle with native pepper.

—— Serves 2 ——

Poached Salmon
—— with Cream Sauce and Blanched Warrigal Spinach ——

For me, one of the best ways to cook salmon is to poach it — it results in a fish so moist and healthy.

Initially, I used a heavy-duty frying pan, until one day I lashed out and bought a stainless fish kettle or poacher. It was such a great investment. Well, that's what I told my husband.

Whilst the fish kettle is also called a poacher, our method of cooking is really steam/poaching. Poaching means a point well below boiling, where the liquid doesn't bubble. With our method, the liquid just bubbles continually. It is important to check the water and add a little more if it's too low.

Now when I have parties, I buy a 2–4 kg salmon and poach it. We usually don't eat all of the fish on the first sitting, but the great part about salmon, is that it's just as tasty cold as hot. And, with its soft orange flesh, aesthetically it looks splendid.

Like most leafy green vegetables, Warrigal spinach has varied uses, but because of the oxides in the spinach, it's important to blanch it and then discard the water.

1 chopped onion
2 bay leaves
2 tablespoons white wine vinegar
water
1 × 2–4 kg salmon *(dependent on people to serve)*
1 large fish kettle or poacher
1 cup thickened cream
⅓ cup white wine
a dash of Tabasco
freshly ground pepper
salt
sufficient Warrigal spinach for guests *(see supplier list on page 152)*
native lime slices *(see supplier list on page 152)*

Combine onion, bay leaves and white wine vinegar in fish kettle and add sufficient water so that the liquid rises just above the tray the salmon sits on in the kettle. Place salmon on kettle tray.

Bring liquid to the boil, then reduce and cover with lid. Poach for about 3 minutes per kilo. When cooked, turn off heat and leave fish in kettle for ½ hour.

Meanwhile, reduce cream, white wine, Tabasco and seasonings.

Just before serving the fish, blanch Warrigal spinach in water and discard liquid. Keep warm.

Gently lift the fish from tray/strainer, place on serving platter and garnish with native lime slices cut to look like scales. Surround with Warrigal spinach. Reheat the warm and creamy sauce and serve in a heavy glass jug.

—— Serves 6–10 ——

Opposite: Poached Atlantic Salmon

Above: Australian Bream in Clay Fish

Australian Bream in Clay Fish

We are very friendly with a famous Australian show business family, the Newmans, and for them, dinner parties must have a theme, including having their guests prepare their own food.

Guests sit down to their dinner table setting which includes a cutting board, rolling pin, small baking tray, length of tinfoil, mallet, knife, spoon and large serviette. On each cutting board is a ball of earthenware clay, and each guest is required to design a clay fish to cover their fresh meal.

Have a go, even though, as a host, it takes longer to set the table, than to prepare the food. You don't have to go to a lot of expense. Improvise with the utensils. Stuffing for the fish was made beforehand.

Stuffing (dependent on numbers):

capers

finely chopped onions

ground native pepper
(see supplier list on page 152)

salt

seeded and finely chopped red capsicum

finely sliced native lime
(see supplier list on page 152)

For each serving:

1 large piece of lightly greased tinfoil

1 bream

25 g butter

native thyme
(see supplier list on page 152)

1 crushed garlic clove segment

salt

¼ sliced mango

1 hunk of potters' clay
(Use any fine earthenware clay, purchased from a pottery or art supplier)

Skewered vegetables:

onions cut into quarters

large peeled mushrooms cut in half

trimmed squash

skewers
(dependent upon numbers; say 2 per person)

Combine stuffing ingredients and refrigerate. Divide between guests, upon arrival, so they can stuff their own fish. Then put tinfoil on the small baking tray and place fish in centre.

Rub in butter, and sprinkle thyme, garlic and salt over. Garnish with mango and wrap fish securely in tinfoil.

Shape a clay mould over the top of the fish; don't forget to be creative and add gill, fin, mouth, eye, tail and use the back of a spoon to press in the scales.

Lift each fish from individual baking trays and place on a larger one. Bake at about 200°C until the clay is dry to touch, usually between 1–2 hours and remember that the clay cover must be fine.

During the last 45 minutes of cooking, prepared skewered kebabs of vegetables can be placed around the clay fish or grilled separately.

When everything is ready, take from oven; guests smash their own clay fish with a mallet. Gently unwrap the tinfoil.

The host serves the fish on preheated plates. Vegetable kebabs provide the garnish.

Baked Mullet in Banana Leaves
—— and Pan-fried Watermelon, served with Australian Steamed Rice ——

The sea mullet is probably Australia's most common edible food. With its camouflaged olive-green top and silvery sides, it is prolific in the waters of all states except Tasmania. An average sized fish is about 1 kg and 45 cm long. The flesh is excellent and is often smoked, fried or grilled.

Tropical watermelon is a very succulent and open textured fruit. It's delicious cold and presents a juicy alternative when floured and browned. And, it's pleasing to learn that we grow our own rice. In fact, Australian rice is exported to Asia.

You have to know someone who grows bananas so you can use the leaves (or see supplier list on page 152) to fully appreciate this recipe. As an alternative, you could buy some paperbark (see supplier list on page 152).

---

2 average-size mullet

1 finely sliced native lime (alternatively, use a lemon) (see supplier list on page 152)

2 crushed garlic cloves

native peppercorns and salt to taste (see supplier list on page 152)

banana leaves, trimmed and scalded (see supplier list on page 152)

4 drops of eucalyptus/gum leaf oil or lemon myrtle oil (see supplier list on page 152)

water

1 cup Australian rice

¼ fresh watermelon

plain flour

2 tablespoons butter

Buy mullet which is already scaled and cleaned. Slash (4 cm deep) each fish diagonally twice on each side and place lime slices in cavities. Combine garlic, peppercorns and salt and rub over fish.

Sprinkle banana leaves with a little water and two drops per leaf of eucalyptus or lemon myrtle oil. Put fish on top and wrap firmly. Place in 180°C oven (or on a barbecue) and bake for 35–40 minutes, until the skin lifts easily and the flesh flakes.

Meanwhile, bring a saucepan of water to the boil and cook rice according to directions.

To prepare watermelon, remove the skin and cut 1 cm slices into rectangular shapes. Pat dry and place on paper towel.

Just before serving the fish, coat watermelon rectangles with flour, heat butter in a heavy-based pan and fry until light brown.

If you have any leftover banana leaves, place on serving plates and gently lift fish onto new leaf. Drain rice, wash if desired, and serve. Garnish with fried watermelon rectangles.

—— Serves 4 ——

Opposite: Baked Mullet in Banana Leaves

Scallop Souffle
—— with Fresh Tomato Sauce and Pumpkin Seed Flatbread ——

This is a fail-safe fish souffle. Always trim the scallops and remove any intestine or brown pieces. Once this is done, the rest of the preparation is a cinch. It's so easy to make and can be served either hot or cold.

The flatbread is a bit like Italian foccacia — find the recipe on page 148.

400 g finely chopped, skinless tomatoes
25 g butter
1 crushed clove garlic
1 tablespoon tomato paste
¼ cup dry white wine
1 teaspoon sugar
1 level tablespoon dry basil (or 1 dessertspoon freshly chopped)
salt and pepper to taste
400 g dry-shucked scallops with membranes and intestines removed; reserving four for garnish
3 egg yolks
300 ml cream
freshly ground pepper and salt
3 whipped egg whites

Combine tomatoes, butter, garlic, tomato paste, wine, sugar, basil, salt and pepper in a large saucepan and slowly cook, stirring occasionally, until it thickens.

Reserve 4 scallops. Together with the egg yolks and cream, puree the remaining scallops in food processor. Add seasoning and fold through whipped egg whites.

Grease 4 souffle dishes and divide mixture evenly or put the mixture in one large souffle plate. Place dishes/plate in a bain marie (I use a shallow cake pan of water), and cook at 200°C for 15–20 minutes.

Serve each souffle garnished with one reserved whole scallop and a small bowl of homemade tomato sauce alongside.

Complete the presentation with some Pumpkin Seed and Bush Tomato Flatbread (see recipe on page 148) or freshly bought flatbread of your choice.

—————— Serves 4 ——————

Marinated Perch with Goats' Cheese Souffle

The acidic ingredients in this marinade actually do the cooking. If you are serving the meal for dinner, let the fish marinate throughout the day.

As goats' cheese is expensive, we've added a proportion of Australian baked ricotta cheese. This cheese is not only less expensive than goats' cheese, but it also provides extra flavour and volume.

400 g perch fillets
3 juiced native limes (see supplier list on page 152)
¼ teaspoon sugar
¼ teaspoon salt
freshly ground native pepper (see supplier list on page 152)
1½ peeled and chopped tomatoes
2 finely chopped shallots
⅓ cup cider vinegar
⅓ cup green ginger wine
1 tablespoon finely chopped coriander
1 crushed clove garlic
¼ cup olive oil
4 tablespoons butter
3 slices white sandwich bread, crusts removed
1 teaspoon sugar
½ cup milk
½ teaspoon salt
ground native pepper to taste (see supplier list on page 152)
dash of Tabasco
2 eggs
150 g coarsely grated Australian goats' cheese
100 g coarsely grated Australian baked ricotta

With a sharp knife, cut fillets into bite-size pieces and combine fish pieces, lime juice, sugar, salt, pepper, tomatoes and shallots.

In another container, combine cider vinegar, green ginger wine, coriander, garlic and oil. Mix well and pour over fish.

Place bowl in refrigerator for at least 4 hours.

Butter medium souffle dish. Butter one side of the bread slices, sprinkle with sugar and cut each slice into thirds. Whisk together milk, salt, pepper, Tabasco and eggs.

Arrange half of bread, buttered side up, on bottom of dish. Sprinkle with half the grated goats' cheese and ricotta. Repeat procedure. Pour egg mixture over. Let stand at room temperature for about 20 minutes.

Bake for 25–30 minutes, or until bubbling and golden. Serve with bowls of marinated fish.

——— Serves 4 ———

Red Snapper Fillets
—— with Oyster Sauce, Fresh Fungi and Green Capsicum ——

One of the most popular eating fish in Australia, snapper has a delicate flavour and a firm and flaky texture.

Many supermarkets sell containers of Exotic Fungi Mix, which includes Shii-take, Shemeji, Enoki, as well as morels and abalone mushrooms.

25 g butter

1 tablespoon flour

a small bottle of oysters

½ cup fish stock

80 ml cream

salt and pepper

2 snapper

plain flour

1 tablespoon butter

2 tablespoons oil

100 g fresh fungi

1 small green capsicum

40 g butter

salt

freshly ground pepper

To make the oyster sauce, melt butter and flour and cook over gentle heat until golden. Take off heat. Strain liquid from bottled oysters into a bowl, add fish stock and then cream. Combine well.

Gradually blend liquids into flour mixture. Stir until sauce thickens. Season. Keep warm.

Dust fish with flour. Heat butter and oil in large frying pan and add fish. Cook for about 8–10 minutes, or until tender.

Meanwhile, clean the fungi really well and cut lengthwise. Wash, trim and finely slice capsicum. In another pan, heat butter, add fungi and fry for about 1 minute. Add capsicum and salt and heat through.

Add oysters to sauce and quickly heat through.

Drain snapper on absorbent paper and then place, red side up, on preheated plates. Divide fungi and capsicum equally and place alongside snapper. Serve warmed oyster sauce on half of snapper.

—————— Serves 2 ——————

Opposite: Red Snapper Fillets

Marrons with Stuffed Baked Potatoes
—— in Light Lemon Aspen Sauce ——

As sea farms are continually increasing, Australia's aquaculture industry is becoming quite large. Part of this industry provides a variety of crayfish known as marrons.

Not so long ago, many residents of the south-eastern corner of Australia were unaware of marrons. Today, these native freshwater crayfish from Queensland and Western Australia are more commonplace.

Marrons can be substituted for yabbies and vice versa, but whichever you use, it's preferable to buy them alive and cook them yourself.

4 medium potatoes
1 teaspoon butter
1 chopped clove garlic
1 teaspoon tumeric
2 chopped spring onions
2 pureed lemon aspen fruit *(see supplier list on page 152)*
½ cup fish stock
⅓ cup dry white wine
container of water
white wine
6 peppercorns
salt
4 chopped macadamia nuts
butter
salt and ground pepper
2 marrons, *dependent on size (for 4 people)*

Wash and scrub potatoes and place in a 180°C oven for about 40 minutes.

When potatoes are about half cooked, prepare the lemon aspen sauce by melting a teaspoon of butter in a heavy-based pan and virtually dry-frying the garlic, tumeric and spring onions. Fold in pureed lemon aspen fruit and gradually add fish stock and white wine. Simmer very gently until a light consistency. Keep warm.

Bring a large pot of water to the boil. Add wine, peppercorns and salt. While this is re-boiling, prepare the potatoes as follows.

Scoop out a third of each cooked potato and mash it with the chopped macadamia nuts, butter and seasonings. Divide the mixture into four scoops and replace in potatoes. Keep warm.

Drop marrons in boiling water and remove less than a minute after they have risen to the surface: they will have bright red shells. Dunk marrons in cold water.

When coolish, twist the head from the edible tail meat. Divide meat and claws and serve with the light lemon aspen sauce and stuffed potatoes. Garnish with some shell.

——————— Serves 4 ———————

70

Baked Salmon Trout Fillets
—— with Creamy Chardonnay Sauce and Grated Potato Cakes ——

Salmon trout is such a versatile and elegant fish. You can bake, braise, steam, saute, poach or grill it. It requires very little cooking to enhance its delicate flavour and if you want to keep some continually on hand, try our curing recipe in the Entrees chapter.

My family always call these potato cakes 'egg whitebait'. I suppose the name originates from the fact that the long pieces of grated potato look like whitebait. Anyway, now that a lot of households have a food processor, you don't have to spend time hand-grating, so they're much quicker to make.

500 g peeled and grated potato
2 grated medium onions
2 lightly beaten eggs
salt and pepper
2 tablespoons butter
1 teaspoon native thyme (see supplier list on page 152)
50 g butter
4 salmon fillets
½ cup fish stock
¾ cup chardonnay
½ cup whipped cream
chopped parsley
ground pepper

Place grated potato and onion in a large bowl, incorporate some, but not all, of the potato liquid, add eggs and seasoning and mix well.

In a large, hot frying pan, melt butter. Place dessertspoonfuls of potato mixture in pan. Cook until cakes have a golden brown base, turn and cook for another few minutes. When cooked, keep warm in a slow oven.

Mix thyme with butter and spread ¾ over fillets. Brush remaining mix over base of ovenproof dish.

Put salmon in dish and season.

Mix stock and chardonnay and pour about half of this liquid around the sides, but not on top of the fish.

Place in preheated oven 180°C for 12–15 minutes. Timing is dependent on size of fillets, so check during cooking. After 5 minutes, cover fish.

Place remaining stock and chardonnay in small saucepan and reduce. Add seasoning if necessary. When correct consistency, (reduced by about half), add whipped cream and fold through.

To serve, pour warm chardonnay sauce over salmon and place on preheated plates. Serve with potato cakes, and garnish with chopped parsley and ground pepper.

—— Serves 4 ——

Native Thyme

Barbecued Yabbies
—— served with Cream of Horseradish Sauce and Salad of Asparagus ——

There are several species of freshwater crayfish in Australia and the yabby is one of them. Yabbies are prawn-like native crustaceans and they are found in sands, dams, lakes and creeks.

If yabbies are caught in muddy streams or dams, they are usually soaked overnight to wash away muddy flavours. However, some people prefer the natural way of just keeping them alive in clean water until cooked.

Salt must be added to the water that yabbies are boiled in. You can tell when they're cooked, because their shell colour changes from blue to red.

Live yabbies are usually boiled in salted water for three minutes. Like other seafood, they must be only briefly cooked, but if you wish to barbecue yabbies, one to two minutes is sufficient. Over-cooked flesh becomes stringy and unpalatable.

12 reasonably large yabbies

olive oil

1 tablespoon preserved horseradish sauce

½ cup yoghurt or sour cream

dash Tabasco

ground pepper

2 chopped spring onions for garnish

600 g asparagus spears

100 g Australian parmesan cheese, grated

freshly ground pepper

Brush yabbies with olive oil.

For the creamy horseradish sauce, mix preserved horseradish sauce, yoghurt or sour cream, Tabasco and ground pepper together and garnish with spring onions.

Wash asparagus spears and snap off tough ends. Cook in water until just tender. Drain well and keep asparagus in strainer and half cover with saucepan lid.

Throw yabbies on barbecue and cook for about 1–2 minutes. For ease of handling, if skewers are available, gently slide through end of each yabby.

Divide yabbies and asparagus spears onto 4 plates. Top asparagus with grated Australian parmesan cheese and freshly ground pepper. Garnish yabbies with cream of horseradish sauce.

—————— Serves 4 ——————

Opposite: Barbecued Yabbies

Ocean Perch Fillets
—— and Australian Blue Vein Cheese served with Winter Salad ——

Perhaps my husband's favourite, this is a most impressive but very easy recipe. Ocean perch is a wonderfully flavoursome and textured fish, but something like rockling could be used in its place. I like to quickly pan-fry fish, but poaching is just as good.

Australia now has some wonderful exotic and full-flavoured cheese including our own blue vein.

Macadamia nut oil is also splendid and, blended with native lime juice, is an excellent dressing for an ever-popular winter salad.

2 tablespoons oil
2 tablespoons butter
4 finely sliced spring onions
250 g slivered almonds
2 julienne-stripped small carrots
1 finely sliced small capsicum
1 teaspoon butter
1 teaspoon oil
2 perch fillets
1 piece of tin foil
75 g Australian blue vein cheese
a selection of mixed lettuce for 2 people
1–2 tablespoon macadamia nut oil
2 juiced native limes *(see supplier list on page 152)*
freshly ground pepper

Place half of the oil and butter in pan and saute spring onions and almonds. Remove and place in medium bowl. Add remaining oil and butter to the pan and saute carrot and capsicum for a few minutes. Remove and add to bowl.

Put butter and oil in a pan and quickly sear fish for about a minute on either side.

Heat griller. Gently lift fish from pan and place on a tinfoil-lined griller tray. Cut blue vein cheese in half, place piece on each fillet and grill for about 2 minutes.

While fish is grilling, add lettuce to winter salad pan and fold through macadamia nut oil and lime juice. Add bowl of onions and almonds and quickly heat through.

Place salad on two preheated plates, with fish alongside. Grind fresh pepper over the lot.

—————— Serves 2 ——————

Opposite: Ocean Perch Fillets

Macadamia Crumbed Rockling or Coral Trout
—— served with Orange and Date slices garnished with Grated Ginger ——

When cut into fillets, both of these fish have a thickness to them which works well with the macadamia crumbs. The nut crumbs are heavier than breadcrumbs and are best used on a fairly substantial fillet.

Done in this manner, the fish is scrumptious and filling, so a few lightly pan-fried orange and date slices with freshly grated ginger is a sufficient accompaniment. Alternatively, the fruit and ginger can be served fresh.

125 g packet macadamia nuts	*1 dessertspoon oil*
flour for dusting 2 fish fillets	*1 dessertspoon butter*
salt	*1 teaspoon butter*
freshly ground pepper	*2 skinned and chopped oranges*
1 lightly beaten egg	*2 sliced dates*
2 rockling or coral trout fillets	*freshly grated ginger*

Grind macadamia nuts in a blender.

Place seasoned flour, egg and ground macadamia crumbs in three separate dishes, and flour, egg and crumb each fish fillet.

In a hot, heavy-duty pan heat the dessertspoon of oil and butter, reduce heat a little and add crumbed fillets. Cooking time depends on size of fillets, but about 3 minutes either side is usually sufficient.

When fillets have been turned, heat a second pan with a little butter and stir fry oranges, dates and ginger for 1 minute.

Serve fillets on large preheated plates and garnish with fruit and ginger.

——————— Serves 2 ———————

Oven Baked Barramundi
—— with Sweet Potatoes and Snap Peas ——

Australia, which is often referred to as 'Down-under', has a 'Top End' alive with barramundi. A firm, sweet fish with white flesh, it can be wrapped in paperbark with wild ginger, and baked in an oven or on top of hot coals.

Sweet potatoes are a very underrated food. These tubers have a unique flavour and can be used in soups or souffles, boiled, steamed or baked, or even candied and served with coffee! Whilst you can buy a white-skinned variety, I prefer the look and taste of those with orange flesh. When cooking sweet potato as an accompaniment, select tubers that are as uniform in shape as possible.

2 single-serve barramundi (about 30 cm long)
2 lengths of foil
1 tablespoon per fish of sherry
2 tablespoons per fish of cream
2 sweet potatoes about 12 cm long and not too thick
sufficient snap peas for two people
1 teaspoon oil
1 teaspoon butter
a couple of dobs of butter
salt and freshly ground pepper

Have the fish cleaned and scaled, but ask the fishmonger to leave the heads on.

Cut two pieces of foil large enough to envelope barramundi. Lightly grease shiny side of foil.

Place fish on foil and cover with sherry and cream. Wrap in tinfoil and put on oven tray.

Scrub and rinse sweet potatoes and place on top of, or alongside, foiled fish. Bake at 180°C. Timing will vary according to the thickness of the fish, but about 30 minutes should be adequate. (If sweet potatoes are large, prepare first and place in oven while preparing fish.)

Trim snap peas. When fish and potatoes are close to being served, heat oil and butter in heavy-based pan and toss and quickly heat snap peas. Keep warm.

Serve barramundi in its juices on large, preheated plates. Slit sweet potatoes and fill with dobs of butter and seasonings. Garnish with snap peas.

——————— Serves 2 ———————

Barbecued Salmon Cutlets
—— with diced Mango, Avocado, Native Lime and Coriander ——

Salmon cutlets are not only extremely tasty, they also make a very good first impression. This is because their size and thickness displays, at first glance, the salmon's magic orange flesh, as well as its silver skin.

Aesthetics aside, these cutlets grill or barbecue extremely well. There are two prerequisites for cooking: one is to prevent them drying out, so you must wipe each side of the cutlet with oil, and the other is to ensure even cooking by skewering the ends together.

Most tropical fruits lend themselves to a quick warming in citrus juices. To me, mangoes are a rather exotic fruit, succulent, with a sweet and tangy flavour. Avocado is a more universal, gourmet food. However, if these fruits are not to your liking, experiment with melons, bananas, pineapple or paw paw in this recipe.

4 salmon cutlets
oil
freshly ground pepper
4 little wooden skewer toothpicks
2 juiced native limes *(see supplier list on page 152)*
2 peeled and diced mangoes
1 peeled and diced avocado
2 teaspoons freshly chopped coriander

Rub each cutlet on both sides with oil, add freshly milled ground pepper and skewer the ends of each cutlet together.

Heat oiled barbecue hot plate or grill and place cutlets on top. Take care when turning the cutlets so they don't break. Barbecue until lightly browned and cooked through. They'll be too dry if they're overcooked.

While cooking cutlets, on another hot plate or in a pan over hot plate, heat the lime juice, then add and gently toss the diced fruit and chopped coriander for about 1 minute.

Place each cutlet on a preheated plate. Garnish with fruit and coriander and pour juice over.

—————— Serves 4 ——————

Opposite: Barbecued Salmon Cutlets

MEAT

Meat

Game meats are lean, high in protein
and have very little fat. Perhaps that's because game birds
and animals hop, leap or generally move about more quickly
than sheep and cattle.

Beef cattle and sheep were early arrivals
in Australia and we have never had any hesitation in killing them
for meat. On the other hand, game meats like kangaroo have always
been in plentiful supply, but it was only the Aborigines who initially
realised its nutritional value.

Today kangaroo is sold throughout Australia
and health-conscious consumers are enthusiastic about its low-fat,
low-cholesterol health benefits. In fact, the meat of both the kangaroo
and the smaller wallaby rate among the lowest cholesterol levels
of all red meats.

The emu's lean red meat is classed as poultry
and is high in protein and iron. Its flavour is gamey, yet it exudes
a sweet aftertaste. Because the emu is flightless, its small wings
don't develop muscle for breast meat. A hind-quarter of emu can
be roasted or sliced into steaks, whilst the drum can be
slithered or cut into fillets.

Most of us are keen to keep our distance
from a living crocodile, but don't hesitate to try some of its
meat. A crocodile steak is virtually fat free and has a centre bone.
When char-grilled it looks like chicken, has a similar colour and
flavour to pork and a texture not unlike tuna.

Water buffalo, introduced to Australia
in the early 1800s, is also lean but like other game meats far more
is exported than eaten within Australia. It's a pity, because that means
the buffalo that's left for Australian consumption fetches quite
high prices. However, it's certainly worth trying buffalo
with our riberry sauce recipe.

But whatever the meat, the key factors are taste, nutrition, quality and
easy preparation.

Happy Aussie eating!

Rump Steak and Onion Rings
—— on the Barbecue served with Mushroom Sauce ——

Alistair Punshon devised this recipe for workers in any field who need a replenishing meal after expending an enormous amount of energy. Choosing grain-fed steaks adds further nutrition.

A duxelle, or reduced preparation, of cooked, mushrooms can be made beforehand.

½ tablespoon butter
½ tablespoon oil
about 12 medium, finely sliced mushrooms
1 medium, finely sliced onion
2 teaspoons basil
½ cup Madeira
200 ml thickened cream
oil for hot plate and onions
4 grain-fed rump steaks
6 medium, sliced onions

Make mushroom sauce by heating butter and oil in pan and adding mushrooms, onion and basil. Gently cook until soft. Add Madeira and cream and reduce. Keep warm.

Heat barbecue hot plate and rub with oil. Sear steaks on both sides and cook to your satisfaction.

Place onion slices alongside steaks, brown and turn until cooked.

Place steaks in centre of four plates and half cover each with mushroom sauce.
Garnish with fried onions.

—————— Serves 4 ——————

Aussie Kangaroo Pie

Australians love their meat pie and sauce, and sporting enthusiasts in particular look forward to eating their lunchtime pie, as much as seeing their heroes succeed. But for them, it's not a real pie unless the top is smothered in tomato sauce.

As an alternative to these commercial pies, we believe that a homemade Kangaroo Pie is a must for any Australian cuisine. A family homemade Aussie Kangaroo Pie has much less fat than a regular beef pie — you'll notice when the meat is sauted there's no excess fat to drain.

But we agree as with any meat pie, the garnish should be red and saucy!

500 g minced kangaroo topside
(see supplier list on page 152)

1 onion

1 cup meat stock

1 cup frozen peas

½ cup tomato sauce

pinch nutmeg

salt and pepper to taste

2 tablespoons flour, blended with a little water

375 g packet shortcrust pastry, thawed

1 sheet ready rolled puff pastry, thawed

tomato sauce or Bush Tomato Chutney
(see supplier list on page 152)

Saute the mince and onion in a frying pan until brown. Add the meat stock, frozen peas, tomato sauce and seasonings. Stir and simmer for 10 minutes. Stir in blended flour and thicken mixture. Allow to cool.

Lightly grease a 23 cm deep pie dish and line with the shortcrust pastry. Moisten the edges with water and spoon in the cold meat mixture. Top the pie with puff pastry, pressing down gently to seal the edges together.

Trim and pinch the edges, brush pastry top with lightly beaten egg and make a small slash in the centre of the pastry.

Bake at 230°C for 10 minutes, then reduce heat to 180°C and bake a further 30 minutes.

Garnish with tomato sauce or Bush Tomato Chutney.

——— Serves 4–6 ———

Aussie Kangaroo Pie

Crocodile Mornay
—— served with Warrigal Spinach and Bush Tomato Chutney ——

The Flamin' Bull Bushfood Restaurant in Warragul, Victoria serves a very popular dish which is similar to this recipe. One of the owners, Rod Short, found crocodile to be a little bit on the dry side until he experimented with a mornay sauce. For the same reason, some Italian restaurants now include crocodile in a moist risotto.

Warrigal spinach was used by Captain James Cook as a tonic for scurvy and is regarded as the first Australian food plant to be cultivated in Europe. Cook's botanist, Sir Joseph Banks actually took spinach seeds back to England, where it is now grown as a summer green. Two hundred years later, Australians are just realising its value!

This native spinach is found along the eastern seaboard and because it's high in oxides, it must be blanched before eating.

Bush tomato chutney is a great garnish, but it's worth buying a few bush chutneys, sauces and relishes and experimenting with these new flavours yourself.

white wine for marinade
1½ tablespoons butter
1½ tablespoons oil
3 crocodile steaks (see supplier list on page 152)
6 tablespoons butter
6 tablespoons flour
3¼ cups milk
seasoning to taste
1 cup grated Australian cheddar
300 g Warrigal spinach (see supplier list on page 152)
Bush Tomato Chutney (see supplier list on page 152)

If you have time, marinate crocodile steaks in a little white wine until the wine becomes slightly gelatinous.

Place butter and oil in a hot pan and, when sizzling, add crocodile steaks. Sear quickly on both sides. Add gelatinous wine and cook steaks on both sides for a few more minutes. Cool.

To make the mornay, melt the butter and gently mix in flour. Gradually add milk and seasoning until the sauce thickens.

Let mixture stand while grating the cheese and then add half the cheese to the sauce mixture. Return to very low heat and stir occasionally.

Finely cut crocodile meat away from the bone and add to mornay sauce. Place crocodile mornay in a greased casserole dish, cover with remaining ½ cup of cheese.

Bake at 200°C until golden brown.

Meanwhile, blanch spinach in water for a couple of minutes, drain and throw away water.

Serve crocodile mornay atop a bed of Warrigal spinach, with a garnish of Bush Tomato Chutney.

—— Serves 4 ——

Above: Crocodile Mornay

Marinated Steaks of Venison
—— in Gin and Juniper Sauce served with Red Cabbage and Baby Corn ——

Venison is sold throughout Australia. The Denver cut and saddle of venison are best for roasting. In this recipe we've used rump steaks of venison, but fillets can also be used.

Because venison is so lean, it's important to retain the moisture by rubbing the steaks with oil before cooking.

2 finely chopped shallots
1 teaspoon oil
1 teaspoon butter
a small packed cracked juniper berries *(see supplier list on page 152)*
2 nips gin
a little water
2 venison rump steaks rubbed with oil *(see supplier list on page 152)*
1 tablespoon oil
¼ finely sliced red cabbage
6 baby corn

To make the sauce, saute shallots in oil and butter, add cracked juniper berries, gin and a little water. Allow this mixture to reduce to an ideal consistency.

In a heavy-based frying pan, sear steaks in the oil and cook for a further three minutes on each side. Keep warm.

Meanwhile, bring half a saucepan of water to the boil. Add cabbage and simmer until just soft. Then bring half a smaller saucepan of water to the boil and cook baby corn.

To serve, place steaks on two large plates and spoon sauce over. Garnish with red cabbage and baby corn.

—————— Serves 2 ——————

Kangaroo Fillets
—— with Stir Fry Snap Peas and Illawarra Plum and Chilli Sauce ——

With such low cholesterol, low fat and high protein, kangaroo fillets are such a healthy, filling and quick meal. The kangaroo side fillet is a perfect size for a steak and is slightly larger than the back fillet which is cut into medallions.

If you are extremely adventurous, you can make your own Illawarra Plum and Chilli Sauce from our recipe in this book (see page 40). Alternatively, check our supplier list on page 152 then lash out and buy some.

250 g snap peas	*1½ tablespoons butter*
4 kangaroo fillet steaks *(see supplier list on page 152)*	*salt*
virgin olive oil	*1 tablespoon water*
ground peppercorns	*Illawarra Plum and Chilli Sauce* *(see recipe on page 40)*
1½ tablespoons oil	*red pepper strips (optional garnish)*

Opposite: Kangaroo Fillets

String the snap peas and place them in icy water.

Simply oil and pepper the fillets and, if you have the time, leave to marinate until ready to cook.

Experts have two schools of thought on the final cooking of kangaroo fillet, but both initially sear the fillets in oil and butter on each side in a very hot pan. You can either turn to a medium heat and cook for about 3 minutes or place your pan in a very hot oven for 4 to 5 minutes. Both methods result in a delicious, medium-rare fillet.

Once cooked, rest the fillets and prepare the snap peas.

Drain peas. Heat oil in a non-stick pan. Add snap peas, salt and a tablespoon of water and stir fry for a couple of minutes until peas are bright green.

Serve immediately with fillets and Illawarra Plum and Chilli Sauce. Garnish with red pepper strips if desired.

——————— Serves 4 ———————

Aussie Surf and Turf
—— served with Spicy Beer Sauce ——

In many areas of Australia the bush runs down to the ocean. Most Australians are lucky enough to be able to incorporate in their diet welcoming beef steak, with tantalising king prawns. In popularity, beer-drinking would be right up there with such a tasty diet, so an accompanying Spicy Beer Sauce is really acceptable.

Alistair Punshon devised this recipe.

2 tablespoons butter
1 onion, sliced
1 clove garlic, finely chopped
chopped chilli pepper to taste
salt and pepper
200 ml cream
200 ml beer
2 beef tenderloin steaks
2 tablespoons oil
1 teaspoon oil
1 teaspoon butter
1 tablespoon native lime juice
(see supplier list on page 152)
seasoning
4 king prawns

Make the beer sauce by heating butter in pan and gently frying onion, garlic and chilli. When onion is soft, add seasoning, cream and beer. Stir and reduce to sauce consistency.

Grease hot plate with 2 tablespoons oil, heat and quickly sear steaks on both sides. Reduce temperature slightly and cook to required taste.

Meanwhile, in heavy-duty pan, add a little oil, butter, native lime juice and seasoning and quickly fry prawns until red.

On two preheated plates, arrange steak with beer sauce over and garnish with prawns.

—————— Serves 2 ——————

Native pepper leaves

Opposite: Aussie Surf and Turf

Pan-fried Kangaroo Swags
—— with Port Sauce and Munthari Kakadu Glaze ——

For this recipe we've added to the gamey tang of kangaroo meat the more subtle flavours of some of Australia's native fruits.

Kakadu plums are one of the three native plums which are being widely used in Australian cuisine today. (The other two are Davidson and Illawarra plums.) The Kakadu plum is the most nutritious of the native plums containing the world's highest fruit source of vitamin C. While muntharies, which are small, apple-flavoured, furry berries, are found along the South Australian sand dune area.

2 kangaroo fillets
(see supplier list on page 152)

1 medium chopped onion

1 tablespoon port

2 teaspoons oil

2 teaspoons butter

1½ tablespoons oil

1½ tablespoons plain flour

2 cups rich meat stock

1 tablespoon tomato paste

1 teaspoon mixed herbs

1 teaspoon grated orange peel

3 tablespoons Australian port

8 sheets of fillo pastry

softened butter

1 tablespoon oil

1 tablespoon butter

1 lightly beaten egg

1 jar Kakadu plum jelly
(see supplier list on page 152)

1 cup muntharies, cooked
(see supplier list on page 152)

Finely dice kangaroo fillets and slice onions. Place together in bowl and pour one tablespoon of port over ingredients. Heat the oil and butter in heavy-duty pan and quickly sear meat and onion.

Make sauce by heating oil in heavy-duty saucepan and blending flour. Gently cook until brown and remove from heat. Carefully mix in stock. Return to heat and add tomato paste, mixed herbs, orange peel and port. Stir in kangaroo and onions, half-cover and simmer gently for about 15 minutes. Cool.

Cut 16 sandwich-plate size (14 cm) circles from fillo pastry and brush lightly with softened butter. Make 8 pastry bases by joining two circles for each base.

To make swags, overlap side lengths, then fold top and bottom flaps securely. Heat a heavy-duty pan and add oil and butter. Dip swags in egg and quickly pan-fry until pastry is cooked. In a separate pan add Kakadu plum jelly and heat through with the muntharies.

Divide munthari glaze between four preheated plates and place one or two kangaroo swags on top of each.

—————— Serves 4 ——————

Crocodile Steaks Pan-fried
—— served on Sweet Potato with Mango Chutney ——

There are two species of crocodile living in the wild in Australia. The saltwater crocodile roams along the northern Australian coastline and in coastal rivers, creeks and swamps. Freshwater crocodiles occur in northern Australian river systems. Both species are being farmed for a now-flourishing food industry.

The main crocodile eating piece is the bulk of the tail. The steak has a centre spine and the fillet comes off this bone.

1 fairly large sweet potato
2 medium-sized lemons
2 crocodile steaks
lots of ground pepper
2 tablespoons virgin olive oil
1 tablespoon butter
mango chutney

Wash sweet potato, leave dripping and place in pre-heated oven at 180°C for about 25 minutes.

If you own a microwave, then sweet potato cooking is far easier. Simply wash and place potato in microwave for approximately 15–20 minutes. When cooked, the potato skin sags and you can feel the soft pulp.

Squeeze lemons and rub juice on either side of each steak. Grind pepper over steaks.

Heat oil and butter in pan and sear steaks quickly on either side. Reduce heat to medium and cook another two minutes on both sides. Turn off heat.

Remove sweet potato from oven or microwave and slit skin lengthwise. Add a little butter, before scooping out potato. This pulp should be soft and won't require mashing.

Place potato in centre of plate and top with crocodile steak. Garnish with mango chutney.

——————— Serves 2 ———————

Kangaroo Pot-of-Gold Pasties

These mixed vegetable and kangaroo Pot-of-Gold Pasties are far easier to prepare than Australian gold now is to find. Australian miners carried their gold in little bags tied about two-thirds of the way up the bag. My niece, Yvette, and I have discovered that pastry bags bunched together in this manner are a rather tasty gold-mine too.

If you prefer to make your own pastry that's fine, but after a day's work, I'm very happy to take six sheets of shortcrust from my freezer and thaw.

While we have found the following ingredients successful, it's fun to experiment with other vegetables. Vegetables vary considerably in size, so just estimate six good handfuls of mixed vegetables.

2 medium carrots
1 stick celery
3 medium potatoes
1 medium turnip
250 g kangaroo mince *(see supplier list on page 152)*
2 medium chopped onions
2 teaspoons chopped parsley
1 teaspoon salt
ground pepper
1 tablespoon water
6 sheets shortcrust pastry (thawed)
spring onion blanched ties
milk or egg for brushing pastry

Simply grate or finely dice all the vegetables and thoroughly mix with kangaroo mince, chopped onion, parsley, seasonings and water.

Place a good-sized handful of mixture in the middle of each pastry sheet.

Draw surrounding pastry into centre and scrunch pastry above mixture. Tie with spring onions. Let the top of the pastry flop over the tie.

Repeat for remaining pastry sheets. Brush each bag of gold with a little egg and milk, or milk only. Bake at 200°C for 30–40 minutes.

——————— Serves 6 ———————

Opposite: Kangaroo Pot-of-Gold Pasties

Braised Wild Boar in Red Wine Gravy
served with Small Potatoes, Illawarra Plum and Chilli Sauce
—— and Aussie Beer Bread ——

This is simple to prepare but once in the oven allow a couple of hours for the dish to cook. Meat stock can be used instead of red wine and water.

Game pig meat has a distinct and strong flavour and fetches higher prices than domestic pork.

Game meats conjure up ideas of basic, hearty meals of meat and spuds; our wild boar with potatoes is typical.

500 g wild boar
(see supplier list on page 152)

plain flour for dusting

salt and pepper

3 tablespoons oil

3 tablespoons butter

3 large chopped onions

1 large diced carrot

2 bay leaves

2 sprigs of thyme or rosemary

ground pepper or 4 pepperberries
(see supplier list on page 152)

red wine

water (optional)

8 small potatoes

½ cup Madeira

Illawarra Plum and Chilli Sauce
(see recipe on page 40)

parsley, chopped finely

Cut wild boar into small chunks and dust with flour and seasoning. Heat heavy-based pan, add half the oil and butter and saute meat. Remove meat from pan and add remaining oil and butter. Saute onions.

Into a large, greased baking dish or casserole, add onions, meat, carrot, herbs and ground pepper or pepperberries. Cover ingredients with red wine, or a mix of half red wine and half water.

Cover dish and bake at 180°C for one hour. Reduce temperature slightly, add potatoes and cook for at least another hour. If the liquid reduces below the meat, add extra wine or water. If you feel energetic while waiting for the boar to cook, you could enjoy making our Aussie Beer Bread to accompany this unusual and tasty meal — see the recipe on page 150. Alternatively, you could sit and read this book until five minutes before serving time, when you'll have to add the Madeira. That would also be a good time to butter the freshly made beer bread or toast your usual staple.

Use large plates and serve this braised boar and spuds in a robust fashion. Serve with Illawarra Plum and Chilli Sauce and sprinkle with lots of chopped parsley: it will still be hearty! And remember, the sensible and wholesome thing to do is to dunk your bread in the gravy!

—————— Serves 4 ——————

Emu Medallions

—— and Sweet Lemon Myrtle Chilli Sauce with Damper Balls ——

When the Western Australian Department of Agriculture conducted fried emu taste-testings in two supermarkets, 91% of people thought the emu was as good as or better than the grilling steak that they were currently buying. Eighty per cent said they would buy the meat at least once a month.

In the above taste-tests, 44% considered that emu tasted like beef and 44% (not necessarily the same 44%!) described the flavour as rich or tasty.

Emu meat is now available throughout Australia and recently I had it served to me with Asian spices in a Chinese restaurant. I love its gamey flavour and the fact that it has a low fat content. This is a fun and easy recipe.

500 g flour
1 teaspoon salt
1 teaspoon bicarbonate of soda
2 tablespoons butter, grated
300 ml milk
2 teaspoons butter, grated
2 teaspoons oil
8 emu medallions
1 jar of sweet lemon myrtle chilli sauce (see supplier list on page 152)

To make the damper — sift flour, salt and soda into large bowl. Rub grated butter into flour mix. Pour in milk and knead the dough into 6 balls. In preparation for rolling, dust the balls with flour.

Roll damper dough into 3 cm diameter balls. Place on greased and floured baking sheet and brush with a little milk. Bake for 25–30 minutes at 220°C. The damper looks and tastes better if you baste with extra milk during cooking.

Five minutes before damper is ready, heat butter and oil and quickly sear medallions in pan or wok until brown. Place the meat in oven with damper for 2 minutes. Take the emu from the oven and rest it for 5 minutes.

Serve emu medallions with sweet lemon myrtle chilli sauce and a damper ball. It's a good idea to have plenty of butter on the table. When guests break open their damper ball, it's great to be able to spread the butter thickly enough so it melts out on to their plate.

—— Serves 4 ——

Kangaroo Meatballs baked in Tomato Sauce
—— topped with Australian Cheddar and served with Ribbon Pasta ——

Australians often buy flattened meatballs or burgers for a warming and quick meal on-the-run. Homemade kangaroo meatballs are easy to make and while they're baking you have time to grate the cheese topping and cook a favourite ribbon pasta.

The tomato sauce keeps the meatballs moist, but if you're not a tomato sauce freak, then use tomato soup or chutney. When cooked, the meat-flavoured sauce is just about fat-free and a hearty new taste sensation.

300 ml tomato sauce

¼ cup water

500 g minced kangaroo topside
(see supplier list on page 152)

1 onion grated

1 teaspoon soy sauce

1 teaspoon Worcestershire sauce

1 teaspoon green ginger, grated

1 teaspoon lightly beaten egg

pepper

flour for dusting meatballs

200 g Australian cheddar cheese, grated

200 g flat ribbon pasta

Pre-heat oven 180°C.

Lightly grease a baking dish, mix tomato sauce and water, and add to the dish.

Thoroughly combine minced kangaroo, onion, soy sauce, Worcestershire sauce, grated ginger, beaten egg and seasoning. Shape into 4 cm balls and dust with flour. Place balls in sauce mix and bake for 20–25 minutes, remembering to turn meatballs halfway through cooking. If the tomato sauce reduces too much, add a little more tomato sauce and water mix.

Grate cheese and, five minutes before serving, top meatballs with cheese.

Cook ribbon pasta according to directions — timing it to be served with the meatballs.

——— Serves 4-6 ———

Buffalo Medallions
and Native Lime Mustard Sauce served with Asparagus and Potato Gratin

Buffalo is an example of where more meat is exported than eaten in Australia. It comes from the Northern Territory and is similar to beef in taste and texture, although slightly saltier. It's certainly worth trying.

If you have time, marinate the medallions for up to two days, then prepare, cook, eat and enjoy!

8 buffalo tenderloin medallions
(see supplier list on page 152)

1 small onion, sliced

1 small carrot, diced

12 crushed peppercorns

2 teaspoons chopped fresh thyme

2 teaspoons chopped fresh chives

200 ml red wine

400 g potatoes

lots of water

salt

40 g butter

40 g grated Australian Cheddar cheese

salt

pepper, freshly ground

nutmeg, grated

200 ml cream

pepper and salt

2 tablespoons oil

3 teaspoons mild mustard

1 tablespoon finely chopped basil

2 tablespoons lime juice

50 ml white wine

½ cup meat stock, preferably veal

1½ tablespoons thickened cream

30 g butter

fresh asparagus — enough for four serves

Place buffalo in flat dish, add sliced onion, diced carrot, peppercorns and herbs. Pour over red wine, cover and refrigerate for up to 2 days or as long as possible.

Wash, peel and slice potatoes into 4 mm slices. Boil in lots of water and a little salt for about 5 minutes. Drain.

Brush a baking dish with soft butter. Layer, by overlapping potatoes in one direction, and cover bottom of dish. Sprinkle with grated cheese, salt, freshly ground pepper and finish with grated nutmeg. Pour cream over everything and bake in preheated oven at 190°C for 20–25 minutes.

When ready to cook the buffalo, pat it dry and season with pepper and salt. Heat oil in heavy-duty pan over medium heat. Add medallions and fry until cooked to your taste. Remove and keep meat warm, but don't clean the pan.

To make the mustard sauce — using pan meat was cooked in and over a high heat, add mustard, basil, lime juice, wine and stock. Stir occasionally until mixture reduces by about one-third. Add cream and further reduce. Add the cold butter and whisk well under sauce. Remove from heat: keep warm.

Boil water in saucepan and trim asparagus stalks from base until knife cuts easily. Discard tough offcuts. Add asparagus to boiling water and quickly blanch so that it remains green and tender. Drain.

Place 2 medallions on each serving plate and cover one medallion with mustard sauce. Garnish with crusty potato gratin and drained asparagus spears.

——— Serves 4 ———

Crocodile Hamburgers
—— on Macadamia Toast with Munthari Sauce ——

Hamburgers are still a very popular Australian meal or snack. Game meats are excellent for making hamburgers, because their low fat content doesn't cause pan-cooking shrinkage. However, to keep any hamburger moist, it's a good idea to include some oil or thick cream.

I like a fairly plain hamburger without too many herbs and elaborate ingredients. But remember, hamburgers must be cooked on a high heat; this forms the brown, crusty outside and seals in the juices.

Many chicken recipes can be adapted for crocodile meat. Basil is tasty in this hamburger recipe and it was included, because basil mixes well with tomato and in turn, tomato and chicken combine well. Oregano could also be used.

You can use your favourite bread or bun for these hamburgers, but if you're feeling rather energetic, homemade, warm macadamia bread is worth the effort — *see our recipe on page 144.*

Muntharies are small, apple-flavoured furry berries, also known as emu apple or native cranberry. They grow as a ground creeper along the South Australian sand dune area. *(See supplier list on page 152.)*

500 g finely chopped or minced crocodile fillets
(see supplier list on page 152)

2 small, chopped mushrooms

pinch basil, fresh or dry to taste

1 egg

1 tablespoon plain flour

2 tablespoons finely chopped onion

2 tablespoons thick cream or oil

½ teaspoon salt

ground pepper

oil and butter for cooking

macadamia bread
(see our recipe on page 144)
or your own bread choice

munthari sauce
(see supplier list on page 152)

With the exception of the oil and butter for cooking, mix and knead all ingredients well. With damp hands, form the mixture into four large or eight small hamburgers. Cook in butter and oil in a heavy-based pan.

Meanwhile, toast and butter two slices of bread (macadamia if you've made some) for each person. Liberally cover bread with munthari or your favourite sauce, place hamburgers between slices and start eating.

Don't worry if the sauce runs out of the bread, you can always lick your fingers!

—————— Serves 4 ——————

Above: Crocodile Hamburgers

Racks of Lamb
served with Baby Potatoes, Light Port Sauce and Eucalyptus
—— and Mint Butter ——

Lamb is a very popular meal in Australia and whilst obviously an introduced species, our lamb is as good as any in the world. Cooking meat in the oven is generally associated with roasting and quite a lot of time, so it's great to reduce the oven time with individual serves of lean lamb racks.

Eucalyptus oil, as a food additive, is now commercially available and is very tasty when added to whipped butter. To really enhance the lamb cutlets, Alistair Punshon suggests adding some mint jelly.

4 lean racks of lamb, each containing 3 cutlets

3 cloves garlic

½ teaspoon dried rosemary

½ teaspoon dried thyme

½ cup white wine

12 baby new potatoes

125 g softened whipped butter

2–3 drops eucalyptus/gum leaf oil (use only food grade)
(see supplier list on page 152)

1 teaspoon mint jelly

salt and pepper to taste

green food colour (optional)

2 shallots

1 teaspoon oil

1 teaspoon butter

4 tablespoons meat juices

2 tablespoons port

Ask your butcher to trim lamb of excess fat. Peel garlic, cut into thin slivers and insert at random into cutlets. Sprinkle racks with herbs and wine.

Wrap a little bit of foil around the exposed bones to prevent them charring. Bake at 190°C on an oven rack with a tray underneath to catch the drips. Cooking time is about 25 minutes for rare, 30 minutes for medium and 35 minutes for well done.

Meanwhile, wash potatoes and boil for about 12 minutes, until tender.

To make the eucalyptus and herb butter: combine whipped butter with eucalyptus oil, mint jelly and seasonings. If you use the green food colour, be careful to add just a few drops to obtain an enhanced eucalypt colour.

Just before serving, scoop out herb butter and make four leaf shaped moulds.

To prepare light port sauce, saute the shallots in a little oil and butter. When the lamb racks are cooked, remove some of the meat juices, add the port and reduce to a light sauce.

Place a little light port sauce under each lamb rack and serve with potatoes alongside. Garnish lamb with a Eucalyptus and Mint Butter leaf mould.

—————— Serves 4 ——————

Opposite: Racks of Lamb

Kebabs of Venison
—— in Riberry Wine Sauce ——

Like kangaroo, venison or deer meat, is low in fat, low in cholesterol and high in protein. Tradition has always been that wild venison is marinated before cooking. However, with farmed venison this is not necessary, although marinades can still be used to complement dishes.

Due to the low fat level in the deer's muscle tissue, venison must never be cooked until it is 'well-done'.

For this meal you need to allow about three hours to make your own riberry sauce. However, if riberries are not available, buy some rosella flowers (see supplier list on page 152) and add a few pinches of herbs, such as cinnamon and ground clove to taste. Rosella flowers are a good alternative to riberries.

500 g venison topside
(see supplier list on page 152)

300 ml low-fat plain yoghurt

ground native peppercorns
(see supplier list on page 152)

finely grated rind and juice of one orange

1 small bunch oregano

1 packet de-stoned Kakadu plums
(see supplier list on page 152)

4 metal skewers
(If wooden skewers are used, soak in cold water for 30 minutes or so to stop them charring when used on the barbecue.)

500 g venison bones

1 tablespoon butter

1 tablespoon oil

250 ml red wine

½ diced onion

1 small packet riberries
(see supplier list on page 152)

2 tablespoons flour

125 ml water

juliennes of orange peel

Cut venison into 3 cm cubes. Combine yoghurt, peppercorns, orange rind and juice and oregano, add the cubed meat and coat it well with the marinade. If you have the time, leave the venison marinating for a day or two, covered, in the refrigerator.

When cooking kebabs, discard excess marinade and alternately thread meat and Kakadu plums on four skewers. Grill or barbecue kebabs for about 10 minutes. Turn frequently.

To make your own riberry sauce, roast the venison bones with butter and oil in a 180°C oven until brown. Add ½ the red wine, onion and riberries and sprinkle with flour. Return to oven and cook for at least another hour.

Add remaining red wine and water to the dish and simmer on top of the stove for another 2 hours, or until the sauce is reduced to your desired consistency.

Pour the riberry sauce over the venison kebabs and garnish with juliennes of orange peel.

—— Serves 4 ——

Opposite: Kebabs of Venison

Above: Wallaby Burgers in Baked Spaghetti Squash

Wallaby Burgers in Baked Spaghetti Squash
—— served with Lavender Mustard ——

Wallabies have a smaller meat yield than kangaroos. Because of this, their meat cuts aren't as thick and are quicker to cook. You only need to sear a wallaby steak on each side and then cook for a further two minutes. Even quicker — check our supplier list on page 152 to find small vacuum packs of smoked wallaby which require no cooking at all.

Wallaby burgers take a little time to make, but are really impressive, especially when served in the squash. It's like eating burgers with pasta, because the flesh of the squash scoops away like strings of spaghetti.

1 spaghetti squash
500 g minced wallaby topside   *(see supplier list on page 152)*
1 small grated onion
1 teaspoon tomato sauce
1 teaspoon Worcestershire sauce
1 teaspoon grated green ginger
4 tablespoons grated Australian cheddar
2 eggs
½ cup chopped parsley
ground pepper
salt
oil for frying
Lavender Mustard   *(see supplier list on page 152)*

Wash spaghetti squash and place in oven at 180°C for ½ hour.

Combine wallaby mince, onion, tomato sauce, Worcestershire sauce, green ginger, cheddar cheese, eggs, parsley, salt and pepper and shape into burgers. Barbecue on oiled hot plate or fry in a little oil in heavy-based pan.

Just before burgers are ready to serve, remove spaghetti squash from oven, cool slightly and cut in half lengthwise. Scoop a little out of each centre and return squash to oven for five minutes.

When the burgers are cooked, remove from pan and place them in the hollow created in the spaghetti squash.

Garnish with lavender mustard.

——— Serves 4 ———

Oyster Buffalo Steaks
—— and Riberry Sauce with Chips and Onions ——

Australia not only has export quality buffalo, but its oysters are also excellent. If you are at all nervous about eating oysters, it's best to eat them smoked or cooked, because heat destroys bacteria.

Riberries, or small-leafed clove-tasting lillypilly fruit, come from rainforest trees and are often seen in northern Australian parks and gardens. Some riberries have seeds, others don't. The seedless are preferred for cooking. Make the sauce from our recipe on page 104.

Restaurateurs tell me that most people expect a large buffalo steak. This recipe really fits the bill.

2 × 5 cm thick buffalo fillet steaks
(see supplier list on page 152)

red wine (optional)

1 crushed clove garlic

2 teaspoons chopped fresh thyme

1 teaspoon prepared French mustard

50 g softened butter

1 can drained smoked oysters

cotton or string for trussing

two large potatoes

four medium onions

oil or butter for hot plate

Riberry Sauce, heated
(see our recipe on page 104)

If you are able to marinate steaks in red wine, from 10 minutes to a couple of hours then you'll reap the benefits. If time doesn't permit, at least make a herb butter by combining garlic, thyme and mustard with the softened butter.

Cut three-quarters of the way through the length of the fillet. Spread half the herb butter on the two fillet centres. Halve the oyster quantity and place on each herb-buttered fillet. Truss the meat securely with cotton or string.

Heat oven to 180°C.

Melt the remaining herb butter in heavy-duty pan over a medium heat, sear and brown steaks on both sides. Transfer liquid and steaks to baking dish and place in oven for a further 15–20 minutes.

Meanwhile, wash, peel and cut potatoes into 10 mm thick chips. Soak in cold water while slicing onions. When onions are ready, drain and dry chips.

Liberally wipe a hot plate or pan with butter and a little juice from meat. Fry the chips on one half and the onions on the other. Sprinkle both with salt and turn constantly.

When ready, serve immediately with oyster buffalo steaks and riberry sauce. A really square meal, where steak knives are advisable.

—— Serves 2 ——

Salad of Smoked Emu Slithers
—— and Lemon Aspen Macadamia Dressing ——

If you have a lifestyle where you are continually planning meals in a hurry, then it's a good idea to keep a smoked drum of emu in your freezer. The drum is small, so it thaws quickly.

By slithering the emu meat and serving it with a tossed green salad dressed with Macadamia Ginger Dressing, your meal will be both extremely tasty and topical.

a mix of lettuce to serve 4 people

1 punnet of cherry tomatoes, washed

Lemon Aspen and Macadamia Dressing
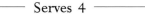
(see supplier list on page 152)

from a smoked emu drum, 12 thin slithers

Wash and drain lettuce mixture and place in salad bowl with cherry tomatoes. Lightly cover with Lemon Aspen and Macadamia Dressing. Gently toss.

Serve lettuce mixture on four plates, drape three emu slithers on each lettuce mound.

—— Serves 4 ——

Kangaroo Rump Roast
—— served with Dobson Potatoes and Queensland Blue Pumpkin ——

This is a hearty roast for the family or for overseas guests who wish to taste a unique meat.

The side and back fillets of kangaroo are best for pan-frying, whilst the rump or legs are excellent for roasting. Have your butcher de-bone if necessary and remove the sinew, gristle and most of the silver skin.

Because there is very little fat on kangaroo, it's important to rub the meat with virgin olive oil. If you have the time, sprinkle freshly ground pepper over the oil and meat and marinate until ready to cook.

Dobson potatoes are grown in Victoria and have beautifully soft flesh. You'll require a very sharp knife to peel the pumpkin, but you'll be well rewarded.

Once I marinated kangaroo roast in walnut oil and peppercorns and it was brilliant. However, because it's important to keep the natural flavour of the kangaroo, don't overdo any marinade with herbs and wines.

I cook roasts in the oven, but some believe a Weber barbecue/smoker is better. Whatever method is used, always remember that you must never over-cook kangaroo. It's best served rare to medium after it has rested for at least ten minutes.

4–6 Dobson potatoes
4–6 pieces pumpkin
2 tablespoons oil
500 g kangaroo rump *(see supplier list on page 152)*
100 ml port or red wine
1 teaspoon blended mustard

Peel potatoes and leave whole; leave skin on pumpkin and cut into large serving pieces and place both potatoes and pumpkin in a roasting pan with oil in a hot oven for ½ hour.

Remove vegetables from roasting pan and turn oven down to 250°C.

Place kangaroo roast in pan and quickly sear both sides. Turn oven to 200°C, return vegetables to pan and cook meat and vegetables for approximately 20–25 minutes.

Rest meat for at least 10 minutes before serving finely sliced kangaroo with vegetables.

While the meat is resting, reduce the roast juices with a little port or red wine and mustard. Spoon over meat.

—— Serves 4–6 ——

Above: Kangaroo Rump Roast

Wallaby Savoury Crepes
—— served with Bush Tomato Chutney ——

Smoked meats are great to have as a delicacy and as a standby. Wallaby is no exception. Combined with the staples of egg, flour, salt and milk you can easily make a light gourmet meal.

Bush tomato chutney contributes an intense piquant flavour to these rather more-ish, savoury crepes.

2 cups flour
½ teaspoon salt
2 eggs
600 ml milk
1 smoked wallaby leg
1 tablespoon chopped parsley
butter
Bush Tomato Chutney *(see supplier list on page 152)*
parsley stalks for garnish

Sift flour and salt and make a well in centre of mixture. Break eggs into well, and, using a wooden spoon, gradually work them into the flour adding half of the milk. Beat well for a minute. Stir in remainder of milk. Allow to stand ½ hour before cooking. This softens the cellulose of the starch grains and produces a lighter batter.

Cut four thin slices of smoked wallaby and finely dice. Add diced wallaby and parsley to batter mixture and pour into a jug.

Heat a heavy-based frying pan and wipe pan with butter. Pour in sufficient batter to just cover the bottom of the pan. Cook until bubbles appear and it turns lightly brown on the base of the crepe. Turn with a spatula or by tossing. Brown crepe on second side.

Place on kitchen paper. Make another three crepes. Place crepes on four warm plates and garnish with bush tomato chutney and stalks of parsley.

—————— Serves 4 ——————

Opposite: Wallaby Savoury Crepes

DESSERTS

Desserts

When creating this chapter, it was obvious
that Australian favourites — Anzac Biscuits, Lamingtons, Pavlova and
Peach Melba — had to be included.

Our next step was to include everybody's favourite —
chocolate, chocolate and more chocolate. But rather than a
chocolate cake, we came up with Aussie Chocolate Damper and
Brandied Muntharies in Terracotta Pots. It's rich and delicious
by itself, or it can be topped with lashings of cream.

By including roasted wattleseeds,
we have also concocted a wonderful and different Chocolate
Mousse, garnished with toasted marshmallows.

Alistair Punshon was very happy to include
his successful Aussie Bush Ice-cream Bombe, which combines
wattle, eucalyptus and honey ice-creams on a
chocolate base.

Because Australians eat litres and litres
of ice-cream every year, we have conceived a light, Midori-green
liqueured Aussie Christmas Ice-cream Pudding, topped with
mangoes frozen in pineapple juice.

The individual Australian Summer Puddings
using Rosella flowers, riberrries, muntharies and raspberries were
adapted from the traditional English berry dessert. For those
who also love a warm pudding, try your hand at the Bunya Bunya
Nut Pudding with Wattle Caramel Sauce.

If you only want a light dessert, then we've made
stewed plums an up-market delight. Port Poached Illawarra Plums
with Australian Mascarpone and Candied Orange Zest is simply
exquisite, while another alluringly colourful stewed plums creation
is our wonderful Lemon Myrtle and Quandong Bavarois Torte.

From our array of 'all things sweet', you can see
that there's a large variety of native foods which are particularly
suited to desserts. As the famous, eighteeenth century French politician
and gourmet Brillat-Savarin once said, "The discovery of a new dish
does more for the happiness of mankind than the discovery of a star."
I hope you enjoy some of these new discoveries.

Port Poached Illawarra Plums
—— with Australia Mascarpone and Candied Orange Zest ——

Alistair and I had a lot of fun devising this dessert. It's really an up-market stewed fruit. You could even liken it to the flavour of German gluwein.

The Illawarra purple/brown plum, also known as brown pine plum, is slightly bitter. The bitterness lessens when cool.

Mascarpone has a thick, wonderfully rich texture that's similar to clotted cream. The orange julienne strips complete the canvas. They are rather splendid when candied, but if time's of the essence, don't bother: just decorate with juliennes of orange zest or peel.

the rind of two oranges
water
1½ cups granulated sugar
5 egg yolks
1 cup sugar
750 g mascarpone cheese
250 g thawed Illawarra plums (see supplier list on page 152)
1 cup port
½ cup water
1 level teaspoon cinnamon
3 cloves
1 cup brown sugar

Illawarra Plums

To make the candied peel, cut the rind from two oranges lengthways into four segments. Cut each segment lengthways into about six pieces and place in a saucepan. Cover with cold water and bring to the boil. Reduce the heat and simmer the rind for 20 minutes.

Drain and reserve 1½ cups of liquid.

Return the liquid to the saucepan and add 1 cup sugar. Stir until sugar has dissolved, add rind and bring to boil. Reduce to simmer and cook for 45 minutes.

Place remaining granulated sugar on a plate. Drain the rind thoroughly, reserving the syrup for other dessert uses. Roll each piece of rind thoroughly in the sugar. Place sugared rind on waxed paper and leave in a warm place until firm and dry. If there is any zest over, store in an airtight container.

For the mascarpone topping, simply beat egg yolks and sugar together until white. Gradually add mascarpone cheese to the mixture and beat until smooth consistency. Refrigerate until required.

If frozen, thaw the Illawarra plums, and add to port, water, cinnamon, cloves and sugar in a large saucepan. Stir continually and bring to boil. Reduce heat, add plums and simmer until plums are soft. Cool.

To serve, divide plums and some liquid between four large plates, add a mascarpone scoop to each and garnish with candied orange zest.

—————— Serves 4 ——————

Aussie Chocolate Damper
—— and Brandied Muntharies in Terracotta Pots ——

Damper is usually thought of as unleavened bread cooked on an open fire. This very basic, staff-of-life recipe consists of a plain flour, salt and water dough, cooked in a camp oven sitting on hot coals. When cooked, it's filling, but fairly plain and ordinary.

Today, self-raising flour often replaces plain flour, and milk replaces water. To make it even more interestingly sweet, we've added cocoa and sugar and some native muntharies.

Muntharies are small apple-flavoured berries, which grow on ground-cover creepers primarily along South Australia's sand dune areas. When muntharies are fruiting, your senses are attracted to the pleasant, apple-smelling sand dunes. They are always available frozen (see supplier list on page 152).

Four small plant-type terracotta pots make wonderful baking containers and provide interesting creations.

500 g muntharies (thawed)
(see supplier list on page 152)
sufficient brandy to cover muntharies
200 g self-raising flour
5 g salt
70 g cocoa
100 g sugar
250 g milk
300 ml whipped cream

Poach muntharies in brandy for 2 minutes. Cool.

Sift the flour, salt and cocoa into a bowl. Add sugar. Add sufficient milk to make a manageable dough.

Line base and bottom half of four terracotta pots with foil and add a loosely-drained tablespoonful of stewed muntharies to each pot. Divide damper mixture equally and add to each pot.

Bake in preheated 200°C oven for 15–20 minutes. Baste with a little milk during cooking.

Cool, up-end on to serving plates and garnish with remaining poached muntharies and whipped cream.

—— Serves 4 ——

Muntharies

Opposite: Aussie Chocolate Damper

Australian Summer Puddings
—— with Rosella Flowers, Riberries, Muntharies and Raspberries ——

This is an adaptation of a traditional English recipe. Apart from the quick poaching of new flowers and fruits, there is no other cooking involved.

The buds of the wild rosella hibiscus have a crispy berry and rhubarb-like flavour. Often called native cranberries, muntharies are small, green and red fruits with a Granny Smith apple flavour. Riberries belong to the rainforest lillypilly family: they are small pink berries with a cinnamon and clove character.

If the native buds and fruits you have are frozen, thaw them first. Raspberries are not only flavoursome, but infuse the ingredients with extra juices.

butter
10–12 slices of day-old white bread, crusts removed
250 g caster sugar
600 ml water
100 g caster sugar
125 g rosella flowers (keeping six for garnishing) (see supplier list on page 152)
100 g riberries (see supplier list on page 152)
100 g muntharies (see supplier list on page 152)
200 g raspberries

Lightly butter six 9 cm stainless steel or glass moulds. Line with bread, overlapping slices and sealing well by pressing edges together. Make sure that there are not any gaps in the bread. The remaining bread will be used for the tops of the puddings.

To make syrup, put sugar and water into a saucepan and heat gently, stirring constantly until sugar is dissolved. Gently toss fruit in extra caster sugar then add rosella flowers (remember to retain six for garnishing) and poach 1 minute. Add riberries to flowers and continue poaching for 1 minute. Then add muntharies and raspberries for another minute. Cool the mixture.

Place lightly drained fruit into the 6 bread-lined moulds and cover puddings with remaining bread. Add small saucer and weight to each pudding to ensure juices are evenly distributed throughout the bread.

When serving, turn puddings out onto individual plates. Garnish each pudding with a rosella flower bud.

—— Serves 6 ——

Rosella Flowers

Above: Australian Summer Puddings

Aussie Christmas Ice-cream Pudding

This is a cool alternative to the traditional plum pudding. It's also great to have on hand when a spontaneous dinner party occurs. With its mango-yellow top and green swirls, guests will be very impressed with your Aussie effort.

As a working woman, I often find it quicker to buy the ice-cream and let it soften. On the other hand, at weekends or holidays, it's fun to be authentic and make your own.

1 diced mango
¾ cup pineapple juice
1 litre ice-cream, softened
200 ml lightly sweetened and whipped double cream
½ cup chopped macadamia nuts
1½ tablespoons Midori
a few drops green colouring

To make your own ice-cream from Alistair Punshon's recipe:

1 cup milk
2 cups cream
3 egg yolks
¾ cup sugar
1 tablespoon glucose syrup
½ cup chopped macadamia nuts
1½ tablespoons Midori
a few drops of green flavouring
non-edible blue gum leaves for garnish
lime topping — optional

In the bottom of a lightly greased pudding bowl, place diced mango and pineapple juice. Freeze.

If using manufactured ice-cream, mix softened ice-cream, lightly sweetened and whipped cream and chopped macadamia nuts in large bowl. Add Midori and a few drops of green colouring. Create large green swirls in the mixture. Place ice-cream mixture on top of frozen mango, level base and return to freezer. Freeze.

If making your own ice-cream, combine milk, cream, egg yolks, sugar, glucose syrup and macadamia nuts, then add Midori and green flavouring and create large green swirls in the mix.

Warm mixture, just like you would an egg custard. Mixture is cooked when you gently blow on the back of your mixing spoon and a rose-like pattern appears. If you have a thermometer, heat to 81°C, then chill and churn in an ice-cream machine. (Or use the alternative method provided in introduction on page 136 for those of you without an ice-cream churn.)

Then as with the purchased ice-cream, place ice-cream mixture on top of frozen mango, level base and return to freezer. Freeze.

To serve your Aussie Christmas Ice-cream Pudding, just wipe bottom and sides of pudding bowl with a warm cloth. Up-end on to a large serving plate and take to the table. It looks rather stupendous actually. Drizzle with lime topping if desired.

Cut into long thin slices and garnish with non-edible blue gum leaves.

——— Serves 8 ———

Opposite: Aussie Christmas Ice-cream Pudding

Bunya Bunya Nut Pudding
—— with Wattle Caramel Sauce ——

The soft, chestnut-like flavour of the bunya bunya nut combines magnificently with the wattleseeds' coffee-chocolate-hazelnut taste. Alistair Punshon's mixing of ingredients is second to none.

200 g butter

1 cup sugar

6 eggs

1½ cups self-raising flour

1¼ cups white breadcrumbs

30 ml golden syrup

125 g bunya bunya nuts, boiled, shelled and finely chopped
(see supplier list on page 152)

150 ml milk

1½ cups apple, peeled and cooked

1 cup sugar

1¼ cups water

1 cup cream

1 teaspoon wattle concentrate
(see page 132 for recipe)

Cream the butter and sugar. Mix in the eggs.

Sift the flour and mix with the breadcrumbs, then add this to the mixture. Fold in the golden syrup, bunya nuts, milk and apple.

Pour the mixture into buttered moulds or one large pudding mould and poach in water. Cooking time is approximately 20 minutes for small moulds and 40 minutes for the large mould.

While the puddings are cooking, put sugar and 1 cup of water in saucepan and heat gently, stirring constantly until sugar is dissolved and sugar syrup is reduced to a golden toffee-like colour. Add ¼ cup of water to stop any over-cooking.

Cool slightly and add cream and wattleseed concentrate. Bring back to boil. Take off stove and cool.

Up-end pudding onto serving plate and pour sauce over.

—— Serves 8 ——

Bunya Bunya Nuts

Opposite: Bunya Bunya Nut Pudding

Quandong and Peach Melbas

This is certainly not a new recipe, but it's a simple enough recipe to allow you to make a comparison test of fruit flavours.

The traditional Peach Melba was named after the famous Australian coloratura soprano Nellie Melba. Born in Richmond, an inner city suburb of Melbourne, Victoria but having lived later in her grand country property at Lilydale, towards the beautiful Yarra Valley to the east of Melbourne, I think she just might approve of both flavours!

Quandongs are native peaches and their red fruits have a tart apricot and peach flavour. If you have the time, they're best stewed and left to steep overnight. To toast macadamia nuts, just place under griller until brown.

Canned peaches may be used.

18 quandong halves
(see supplier list on page 152)

water

½ cup caster sugar

juice of one lemon

cinnamon stick

250 ml water

¼ cup sugar

6 fresh peach halves

12 small rounds of sponge cake

12 dessertspoons peach syrup

12 scoops ice-cream

12 dessertspoons strawberry syrup

300 ml whipped cream

2 tablespoons chopped macadamia nuts, toasted

Soak dried quandongs in water and bring them to the boil with caster sugar, lemon juice and a cinnamon stick. So that the fruit won't discolour, simmer for no longer than 4–5 minutes. To maximize flavours, cool and stand overnight.

To poach the fresh peaches bring water and sugar to the boil. Stir continually. Reduce heat, add peach halves and simmer until just soft. Cool.

Make Melbas by placing a round of sponge cake in each of twelve 9 cm moulds and soak with peach syrup. Place a drained peach half on top of the sponge cake in six moulds and 3 drained quandongs in each of the six remaining moulds. Ensure the hollow sides of fruit is uppermost. (Keep the poaching liquid for other desserts.)

Place a scoop of ice-cream on top of each fruit mould. Pour strawberry syrup over each ice-cream scoop. Garnish with whipped cream and toasted macadamia nuts.

——— Serves 6 ———

Above: Quandong and Peach Melbas

Emu Egg Cinnamon Pavlova
—— with Nougat Cream, garnished with Macadamias and Sugarbark ——

Most of us have heard of world famous, prima ballerina Anna Pavlova, but did you know that a chef in the Melbourne suburb of St Kilda invented the wonderful meringue dessert? Well, our consultant has changed a few ingredients for a native variety!

It's certainly a delicious recipe where an emu egg is the equivalent of 6 or 7 small hen eggs. On the other hand, if you need to use hen eggs, at least the macadamia nougat cream authenticates cooking with an Australian product.

If you separate the emu egg and let it stand overnight, the strong game flavour will be less noticeable.

Pavlova:

white of 1 emu egg, or 4 large egg whites
(see supplier list on page 152)

1 cup sugar

1 teaspoon vanilla essence

1 teaspoon vinegar

1 teaspoon ground cinnamon

Nougat cream:

2 tablespoons Nutella

125 g ground macadamia nuts

300 ml semi-whipped cream

Caramelised macadamias:

1 cup sugar

½ tablespoon golden syrup

½ cup water

100 g macadamia nuts

1 sheet greaseproof baking paper

Sugarbark:

½ cup coffee sugar crystals

½ cup demerara sugar

½ cup caster sugar

Preheat oven to 160°C.

Whisk egg whites to a peak. Add half the sugar and whisk for 1 minute. Add the rest of the sugar, and again, whisk for 1 minute.

Add vanilla essence, vinegar, ground cinnamon, fold, but do not whisk. Shape mixture and bake for 10 minutes at 160°C on a lightly greased and floured baking tray. Turn oven down to 130°C till the pavlova has crust: cook a further 10 minutes.

To make the nougat cream: gently fold Nutella and ground macadamia nuts through the whipped cream.

To caramelise the macadamias: begin by combining sugar, golden syrup and water in a heavy-duty saucepan. Stir, without boiling, until sugar is completely dissolved. Briskly boil, without stirring for about 10–15 minutes, until mixture thickens and is a toffee colour. Take off the heat and quickly dip nuts into toffee. Place each nut onto greaseproof baking paper to cool and set.

To make the sugarbark: in a small bowl combine coffee crystals, demerara sugar and caster sugar. Sprinkle mixture evenly over lightly-greased foil. Place under hot grill until dissolved. (Watch constantly, otherwise sugar may burn.) Cool and break into pieces.

Spread nougat cream on cool pavlova and decorate with caramelised macadamias and sugarbark.

———— Serves 8 ————

Opposite: Emu Egg Cinnamon Pavlova

Anzacs
—— served with Paw Paw Sorbet ——

There are two schools of thought on how Anzac biscuits originated. Researchers at the Australian War Memorial in Canberra, ACT, believe they were not named Anzacs until after The Great War. They suggest it was at this time that Anzacs were devised to sell as fund-raisers for returned soldiers.

However, it is recorded that variations of homemade Anzacs were sent to soldiers of the Australian and New Zealand Army Corps (ANZAC) during that same war.

Anyway, I always feel justified in eating lots of these moreish cookies, because the paw paw sorbet accompaniment is so light.

1 cup rolled oats
1 cup plain flour
1 cup sugar
¾ cup coconut
125 g butter
1 tablespoon golden syrup
1 teaspoon bicarbonate of soda
2 tablespoons boiling water
125 g packet glace cherries — optional
2 litres water
1 kg sugar
1 medium peeled and pureed paw paw

Mix oats, sifted flour, sugar and coconut in large bowl.

Combine butter and golden syrup in pan, stir over low heat until butter is melted. Mix soda and water, add to butter mixture, and then stir into dry ingredients while mixture is warm.

On greased tray, roll heaped teaspoons of mixture into balls and place about 4 cm apart. Press each ball lightly with fork and centre a glace cherry on each Anzac — if you are using them.

Bake in slow oven about 20 minutes or until golden brown. Loosen biscuits while warm; cool on trays.

To make sorbet, put the water and sugar in a saucepan and heat gently, stirring until the sugar has dissolved. Bring to boil, then boil rapidly for 15 minutes, until you have a light syrup. Leave to cool.

Add pureed paw paw to the cooled sugar mixture. Mix well. Pour into two or three shallow freezerproof containers and freeze for 2–3 hours until sorbet is set.

Turn the sorbet out into a bowl and break down the ice crystals with a fork. Return to the containers and freeze until firm, a further 2–3 hours.

Serve the sorbet in chilled glasses with Anzac biscuits.

—— Serves 6 ——

Lamingtons
—— with Native Peppermint Tea ——

Lamingtons are ubiquitous in Australia. These national classics are seen at fetes, fund-raising appeals, cake shops and supermarkets. Why? Because people love them.

Lord Lamington would be delighted to know just how popular his creation has become. As governor of Queensland 1895–1901, he was keen for his cook to find a way to moisten cakes that had dried out in the hot climate.

If you don't have time to make the sponge cake, buy one and leave it for a day or so, or put it in the freezer for about an hour and it will be easier to cut.

So, when you make this recipe, ask a semi-healthy chocoholic friend to share the purity of the native tea with the richness of Lord Lamington's creations!

3 large eggs
½ cup caster sugar
¾ cup self-raising flour
½ cup cornflour
1 tablespoon melted butter
1 tablespoons hot water
3 cups icing sugar
½ cup cocoa
50 g grated butter
¾ cup boiling water (perhaps a little more)
approximately 2 cups desicated coconut

native peppermint leaves
(see supplier list on page 152)

Preheat oven to 200°C.

Beat the eggs until they are light and frothy. Add the sugar and beat again until you have a pale, thick and creamy mixture.

Sift the flour and cornflour on to a piece of paper and then sift it back into the egg mixture. Fold it in until all traces of dry flour disappear.

Stir the butter into the hot water and add to the cake mix, folding it through lightly.

Pour into a greased 20 cm square tin and bake in a pre-heated 200°C oven for about 20 minutes or until the cake is firm to touch on top. It should be shrinking away slightly on the sides.

Leave to cool for 5 minutes then turn out on to a wire rack to completely cool. Leave the cake for a day or until firm enough to cut.

Cut cake into about 20 squares: this depends on how big you want your lamingtons, and then make the icing.

Sift the icing sugar and cocoa into a bowl. Add the grated butter and boiling water. Mix until smooth. Stand this bowl in a pan with some hot water and leave until the icing is runny.

Keep icing in pan of hot water to make it easier when dipping the pieces of cake. After dipping, roll individual cakes in coconut.

Make peppermint tea simply by steeping native peppermint leaves in boiling water. Invite some friends and serve them lamingtons with a refreshing cup of native peppermint tea.

—— Makes about 20 ——

Wattle Chocolate Mousse
—— served with Toasted Marshmallows ——

Chocolate mousse is one of those inevitable desserts that features on the menus of many restaurants. It's a very quick recipe to make for the majority of us who have a fetish for chocolate.

The wattle flavour comes from the roasted seeds of several species of the many wattles found in Australia. The seeds' coffee-chocolate-hazelnut taste combines with the mousse to provide a luscious, creamy texture. The toasted marshmallows add extra colour and fluffiness.

Wattleseed concentrate:

200 ml water

40 g sugar

40 g wattleseeds
(see supplier list on page 152)

Mousse:

3 tablespoons water

100 g cooking chocolate

1 tablespoon caster sugar

2 lightly beaten egg yolks

3 tablespoons wattleseed concentrate (see above)

½ cup semi-whipped cream

2 stiffly beaten egg whites

12 toasted white marshmallows

mint leaves for garnish

To make wattleseed concentrate, you need to bring the water to the boil, add sugar and wattleseeds. Stir until sugar has dissolved and wattleseeds infuse flavour into water; this takes about 5 minutes.

In a bowl over hot water, melt chocolate with water. Add sugar, stir until blended. Cool.

Whip cooled chocolate mixture, gently fold in egg yolks, 3 tablespoons of wattleseed concentrate and cream. Fold in egg whites.

Place marshmallows under griller, or on a metal skewer over a gas flame and quickly toast.

Pour wattleseed chocolate mousse into four, long-stemmed wine glasses and refrigerate. Decorate with toasted marshmallows and mint leaves.

—————— Serves 4 ——————

Opposite: Wattle Chocolate Mousse

Lemon Myrtle and Quandong Bavarois Torte

Sweetened eggs, lemon myrtle leaves and cream in the bavarois are all complementary flavours to the slightly acidic taste of the quandong or native peach. The quandongs could be stewed the day before and just heated when you're ready to serve the bavarois.

Because I usually don't have the time, I often buy my pastry base and cook it while I'm making the bavarois and stewing the quandongs. Of course, if you have the time, make your own short crust pastry base.

8 egg yolks

250 g sugar

600 ml milk, warmed

4 lemon myrtle leaves or 5 ml lemon myrtle oil
(see supplier list on page 152)

30 g gelatin

cold water

vanilla essence — optional

600 ml semi-whipped cream

1 pre-baked sweet short crust pastry base
(or favourite recipe for pastry)

100 g sugar

200 ml water

4 cloves

250 g quandongs
(see supplier list on page 152)

Cream eggs and sugar, add warm milk and lemon myrtle leaves or oil, and cook as egg custard. Mixture is cooked when you gently blow on the back of your mixing spoon and a rose-like pattern appears.

Add gelatin which has been softened in cold water. Strain and flavour with a little more lemon myrtle oil (or vanilla) if required.

When mixture is the consistency of whipped cream, fold in semi-whipped cream. Pour into a 20 cm spring-form cake tin lined with pre-baked short crust base and refrigerate.

Stew quandongs by putting sugar, water and cloves in a saucepan and heat gently, stirring constantly until sugar is dissolved. Add quandongs and simmer until fruit is soft. At this stage the fruit will be slightly acidic and have a plum/peach texture. Cool.

To serve, wipe tin with warm tea towel, unclip spring-form and remove the bavarois. Slice and serve with stewed quandongs.

——— Serves 6–8 ———

Lemon Myrtle Leaves

Opposite: Lemon Myrtle and Quandong Bavarois Torte

Aussie Bush Ice-cream Bombe

This is an elegant ice-cream bombe with a difference and it was completely devised by Alistair Punshon. Its light, heaven-sent taste combines wattle, eucalyptus and honey ice-creams with a scrumptious chocolate cake.

Eucalyptus or gumleaf oil is a special food preparation. Do not be tempted to use normal household eucalyptus, or fragrance oil.

Just a tip. If you don't have an ice-cream churn, you can still make this superb bombe. Place the prepared ice-cream mixes into the freezer, and whip them with an electric mixer at intervals during freezing. Or, alternatively, use readymade vanilla ice-cream.

Wattle concentrate flavouring:

100 ml water

1 tablespoon wattleseed
(see supplier list on page 152)

Eucalyptus flavouring:

100 ml water

1 teaspoon food grade eucalyptus/gum leaf oil (see supplier list on page 152)

1 tablespoon pure bush honey

Ice-cream:

1 cup milk

2 cups cream

3 egg yolks

¾ cup sugar

1 tablespoon glucose syrup

flavourings — as above

To assemble the bombe:

wattle ice-cream

eucalyptus and honey ice-cream

Vienna chocolate cake, bought and sliced

1 packet Ice-cream Chocolate Magic

To make the wattle flavouring, combine the water and wattleseed and bring to the boil, leave to cool and add to a litre of ice-cream.

For the eucalyptus flavouring, combine all ingredients, stir to dissolve the honey and add to another litre of ice-cream.

To make the ice-creams yourself, the quantity of ice-cream mix listed is needed for each flavour. (Or else buy two 1 litre vanilla ice-cream cartons.)

Combine the ice-cream base mix and flavouring. Warm, as you would an egg custard. Mixture is cooked when you gently blow on the back of a mixing spoon and a rose-like pattern appears. If you have access to a cooking thermometer, heat to 81°C.

Chill and churn in an ice-cream machine. (Or use the method detailed in introduction.) Repeat for the second flavouring.

Use 9 cm stainless steel moulds or one large mould which have been chilled in the freezer. Spoon in the wattle ice-cream and shape to form a 2 cm thick shell of ice-cream formed up to the rim. Fill with eucalyptus ice-cream and top the mould with a 10 mm layer of purchased Vienna chocolate cake.

Set each bombe in the freezer.

Wipe moulds with warm cloth and remove bombes. Put Ice-cream Chocolate Magic into a bowl and dip half of each bombe into the chocolate. It sets instantly.

— Makes 8–10 bombes —

Above: Aussie Bush Ice-cream Bombe

BREAD

Bread

Ever thought there must be an alternative
to a Devonshire Tea? We did too, and so Alistair and I would love
you to try our Aussie Tea and Wattleseed Buns with Rosella Flower Jam
and Cream as our Australian alternative.

Before you get to a morning or afternoon tea however,
try the Munthari and Orange Muffins.

Our Pumpkin Scones are great for morning
and afternoon tea get-togethers, or, you might prefer the slightly
sweeter Soda Banana Bread.

Aussie Beer Bread is a great barbecue
and lunchtime loaf while for a more elegant lunch you could
try our Modern Damper in Terracotta Pots.

If flatbreads are your scene, you could
cook our Pumpkin Seed (and Bush Tomato) recipe. When sliced,
toasted and buttered, the Macadamia Wholemeal Bread is also a heart-
warming success.

Whichever recipe you choose to make, butter
and eat, you'll be aptly rewarded. Most people can relate to the line
from A.A. Milne's, *When We Were Very Young* rhyme
'I do like a little bit of butter to my bread':
we still like butter on our bread or toast.

Bread, however, has changed. We've come
a long way from the plain flour damper that our ancestors made.
There's been a very successful blending of old and new
breadmaking techniques.

When you make your bread at home,
you have control and are able to experiment with ingredients.
That makes breadmaking heaps of fun. Even the humble damper can
include ingredients like herbs, grated cheese or bush tomato chutney.

And never be intimidated by the thought
of making your own bread. Once you understand the process, then it's
quite easy and very rewarding.

For aroma and eating, freshly baked bread
is certainly well worth the making.

Modern Damper in Terracotta Pots

Damper is the bush bread of Australia. It is usually thought of as unleavened bread cooked in a camp oven sitting on hot coals. When cooked, it's filling, but fairly plain and ordinary.

In our modern kitchen version, we've replaced plain with self-raising flour, water with milk and suggested you make individual dampers in small, plant-type terracotta pots.

2 cups self-raising flour
¼ teaspoon salt
about 1¼ cups milk, warmed
several mini terracotta pots for baking

Sift the flour and salt into a bowl, add sufficient milk to make manageable dough.

Lightly grease terracotta pots with butter and then dust with flour. Fill each pot with dough. Place pots on baking sheet and cook for 25–30 minutes at 220°C.

Baste tops with milk during cooking.

Aussie Tea and Wattleseed Buns
—— with Rosella Flower Jam and Cream ——

This is our stand against the Devonshire Tea. Not that we have anything against scones and jam. It's just that the Devonshire Tea is English and it's about time we created an Australian equivalent.

So here it is. The tea could be any variety, but we suggest trying lemon myrtle. Infused lemon myrtle tree leaves are not tart, but release a medium-sweet taste with an enticing sweet-lemon aroma.

The wattleseed comes from a mixture of several species of Australian wattle trees and the rosella flower buds from hibiscus bushes.

Cream is always delicious on buns or scones. If you prefer savoury buns at another time, just omit the sugar in the dough.

500 g flour
5 g salt
60 g sugar
7 g dried yeast
15 g honey
250 ml water
10 g wattleseed infused with 50 ml water and then strained (see supplier list on page 152)
50 g butter, grated
milk, for glazing
1 beaten egg, for glazing
1 jar Rosella Flower Jam (see supplier list on page 152)
300 ml whipped cream
lemon myrtle leaves or teabags of mixed native herbs (see supplier list on page 152)

Mix flour, salt, sugar and yeast. In another bowl, mix honey, water and strained wattleseed and then combine with dry ingredients. Knead for approximately 5 to 8 minutes. Add room temperature grated butter and knead for a further 5 minutes until dough is smooth and elastic.

Place in warm room and prove dough until it doubles in size. Knock dough down. Mould into small buns, prove again until buns are double in size.

Glaze with combined milk and beaten egg. Cook at 200°C for 25 minutes.

Cut buns in half, fill with rosella jam and whipped cream. Serve with lemon myrtle leaves steeped in a teapot of boiling water or use teabags of mixed native herbs.

Note: Purchased wattleseed can be made into coffee, by placing one teaspoon of wattleseed into an expresso machine and express as normal coffee. If you froth the milk on top, then you've got a wattlecino!

—— Serves 8 ——

Above: Aussie Tea and Wattleseed Buns

Macadamia Wholemeal Bread

Macadamias are such a versatile nut. They can be used in so many ways, including as a crusty topping for bread. You could even crush extra nuts and blend them into the butter you're going to lash onto the cooked loaf.

This non-yeast, wholemeal bread recipe is a delightful change from lighter breads.

½ cup boiling water

30 g butter

1 tablespoon honey

3 cups wholemeal flour

1 cup wheatgerm

½ teaspoon bicarbonate of soda

1 teaspoon salt

about 1 cup milk — warmed for preference

125 g chopped macadamia nuts

With the water, melt the butter and honey in a saucepan. Cool, and add the remaining ingredients.

Knead to a dough and place in a greased and floured loaf tin. Cook at 230°C for 30–40 minutes or until bread tests hollow by tapping.

Munthari and Orange Muffins

Hot, buttered muffins for breakfast are a delight.

If you want to surprise a friend with such a welcoming morning meal, it's best to prepare the ingredients the night before. Then in the morning you only have to combine and spoon the mixture into tins. Alternatively, make the muffins the day before and heat through in the morning.

Having an apple-like consistency, the native munthari really adds to the flavour and moistness of these muffins.

1 cup bran or crushed cereal

1 cup milk

125 g butter

¾ cup brown sugar

½ grated rind of an orange

1 beaten egg

1½ cups sifted self-raising flour

½ teaspoon salt

1 cup muntharies
(see supplier list on page 152)

Soak the bran or cereal in the milk. Cream the butter and sugar together with the grated orange rind. Add the egg gradually, then the soaked cereal. Fold in the flour and salt and then finally the muntharies.

If muntharies are unavailable — blueberries could be substituted.

Divide the mixture equally between about 16 greased patty or muffin tins. Bake at 190°C for 15–20 minutes.

——— Makes 16 ———

Above: Macadamia Wholemeal Bread

Queensland Blue Pumpkin Scones

It's hard to beat this wonderful savoury scone. This recipe is well-known around Australia and is synonymous with an ex-Queensland Premier's wife, retired Senator Flo Belkje-Peterson.

And people rave about these tasty scones that are so easy to make. Remember to cook and mash the Queensland Blue pumpkin before getting the rest of the scone ingredients together. If you have a microwave, peeled and diced pumpkin cooks quite quickly on a high heat.

Pumpkin scones are simply delicious when buttered hot. They can also be eaten cold or used as a base for hors d'oeuvres — see Entrees chapter.

40 g butter
¼ cup caster sugar
1 lightly beaten egg
250 g cooked mashed pumpkin
2½ cups self-raising flour
½ teaspoon ground nutmeg
⅓ cup milk, approximately
butter to spread on scones — optional
parsley or coriander garnish

Preheat oven to 250°C.

Lightly grease 2 × 20 cm round sandwich pans or cake tins.

Beat butter and sugar in a small bowl with an electric mixer, until light and fluffy. Gradually beat in egg and transfer to a large bowl.

Stir in pumpkin, then sifted flour and nutmeg, and enough milk to make a soft, sticky dough. Turn dough onto lightly floured surface and knead lightly until smooth. Press dough out to about 2 cm in thickness and cut about 5 cm rounds from dough.

Place scones, just touching, into prepared tins. Brush with a little milk. Bake in a very hot oven for about 15 minutes.

Serve with plenty of butter, if desired, and a sprig of parsley or coriander to garnish.

——— Makes 16 ———

Opposite: Queensland Blue Pumpkin Scones

Pumpkin Seed and Bush Tomato Flatbread

*Native bush tomatoes have a tamarillo-like flavour and grow to a marble size.
They grow in central Australia and sometimes shrivel on the shrub,
so they're also known as desert raisins.*

*For cooking they make a good sauce or chutney on their own, or as an additive give
a pungent, tangy flavour to things such as tomato soup or tinned tomato.*

2 teaspoons dried yeast
1½ cups plain flour
½ teaspoon salt
¼ cup warm water
½ tablespoon olive oil
1 egg
75 g roasted pumpkin seeds
bush tomato chutney
(see supplier list on page 152)

Mix yeast with the flour and salt. Add water and knead for 10 minutes. Cover and set aside in a warm place until dough has doubled.

Lightly whisk together the oil and the egg. Punch down the dough, add the egg/oil mix and knead until the dough is smooth and elastic. Mould into a flat, round loaf and press in the pumpkin seeds.

Place on a greased baking sheet, cover in a warm place and allow to rise for about 1 hour; that is, until it does not spring back when pressed lightly.

Bake in a preheated 220°C oven for 10 to 15 minutes. Cool a little. Cut into wedges and spread with bush tomato chutney.

Soda Banana Bread

Australian bananas grow exceedingly well in the warmer north-eastern areas of the continent. They are a meal in themselves and when included in this soda bread, they are even more filling.

Breads can be cooked in a variety of containers, like tins, terracotta pots, camp ovens and metal-handled pans or skillets.

So, in this recipe we used a skillet and remembered to cover the hot handle when we were transferring it from the oven. They're fun to use, but certainly not essential.

6 tablespoons butter
2 cups plain flour
1 cup wholemeal plain flour
1½ teaspoons salt
1 tablespoon baking powder
1 teaspoon baking soda
¾ cup granulated sugar
1 cup mashed banana
1 cup milk
2 well-beaten eggs
1 teaspoon vanilla extract

Smear 2 tablespoons of the butter evenly in a 25 cm cast-iron pan or skillet. Line your buttered pan with waxed paper.

Melt 2 tablespoons of butter in a separate pan. Cool.

Stir dry ingredients together and add mashed banana. Toss well to coat.

Whisk together milk, eggs, vanilla and melted butter. Add to the dry mixture. Mix until blended, but don't overmix.

Spoon soda batter into prepared pan, smooth top and dot with remaining butter.

Bake in a preheated 180°C oven until it is golden brown, puffed and tests hollow when tapped; this takes about 1 hour.

Cut and serve directly from the skillet, or cool slightly before removing from the skillet.

Aussie Beer Bread

Beer bread was an obvious alternative to damper. Bushmen wanted leavened bread, but yeast was not available to them as a rising agent, beer was.

Today, Aussie Beer Bread is served with butter dripping over the sides or with a few drops of edible eucalyptus oil (see supplier list on page 152) mixed into the butter before spreading.

The beer is easier to mix into dough after the froth has dissipated.

3 cups self raising flour
¼ cup sugar
1 level teaspoon salt
¾ × 375 ml can of beer — drink the rest!

Mix all ingredients thoroughly, but lightly. You don't knead beer bread.

Shape the dough into the shape of your choice — round or oblong.

Bake at 175°C for one hour, or until the bread tests hollow by tapping.

Opposite: Aussie Beer Bread

Supplier list

We have not listed suppliers for each fish or seafood species mentioned as many local supermarket fish counters and fishmongers at produce markets and fish markets will generally stock, or be able to order, every species mentioned, depending upon seasonal availability.

banana leaves
- order from your greengrocer

buffalo
- Rossinis Fine Foods and Poultry
- produce markets
- some specialist butchers

bunya bunya nuts
- Bush Tucker Supply Australia
- Gundabluey Bushfoods (Robins Foods brand)
- Robins Foods Pty Ltd
- Tasmanian Wild Foods at Pepper Berry Cafe

bush tomato chutney
- Bush Tucker Supply Australia
- Robins Foods Pty Ltd

bush tomato sauce
- Bush Tucker Supply Australia
- Gundabluey Bushfoods (Robins Foods brand)
- Robins Foods Pty Ltd

crocodile
- Douglas Seafood and Game
- Rossinis Fine Foods and Poultry
- produce markets
- specialist butchers
- some specialist gourmet food stores

emu
- Douglas Seafood and Game
- Rossinis Fine Foods and Poultry
- produce markets
- specialist butchers
- some supermarkets
- some specialist gourmet food stores

emu eggs
- Bush Tucker Supply Australia (only available July-September)

eucalyptus or gumleaf oil
- Bush Tucker Supply Australia

ginger dipping sauce
- Hermans Foods Pty Ltd

ground bush tomato (also known as akudjura powder)
- Bush Tucker Supply Australia

gumleaf (eucalyptus) oil
- Bush Tucker Supply Australia

Illawarra plum sauce
- Robins Foods Pty Ltd

Illawarra plums
- Bush Tucker Supply Australia
- Robins Foods Pty Ltd

juniper berries
- Robins Foods Pty Ltd
- health food stores
- some specialist gourmet food stores

Kakadu plum jelly
- Bush Tucker Supply Australia
- Gundabluey Bushfoods (Robins Foods brand)
- Robins Foods Pty Ltd

Kakadu plums
- Robins Foods Pty Ltd

kangaroo
- Douglas Seafood and Game
- Gundabluey Bushfoods
- Rossinis Fine Foods and Poultry
- produce markets
- some supermarkets
- specialist butchers
- some specialist gourmet food stores

lavender mustard
- Yuulong Lavender Estate

lemon aspen
- Bush Tucker Supply Australia
- Gundabluey Bushfoods
- Robins Foods Pty Ltd

lemon aspen and macadamia dressing
- Australian Native Produce Industries Pty Ltd — Red Ochre Produce

lemon myrtle leaves
- Bush Tucker Supply Australia
- Gundabluey Bushfoods
- Robins Foods Pty Ltd

lemon myrtle oil
- Bush Tucker Supply Australia

lemon myrtle vinaigrette
- Australian Native Produce Industries Pty Ltd — Red Ochre Produce
- Robins Foods Pty Ltd

macadamia dressing
- Australian Native Produce Industries Pty Ltd — Red Ochre Produce
- health food stores
- some specialist gourmet food stores

mixed native herbs teabags
- Bush Tucker Supply Australia

muntharies
- Bush Tucker Supply Australia
- Robins Foods Pty Ltd

munthari sauce
- Australian Native Produce Industries Pty Ltd — Red Ochre Produce

native lime
- Bush Tucker Supply Australia
- Robins Foods Pty Ltd

native pepperberries
- Bush Tucker Supply Australia
- Gundabluey Bushfoods
- Tasmanian Wild Foods at Pepper Berry Cafe

native pepper/corns
- Robins Foods Pty Ltd

native peppermint leaves
- Robins Foods Pty Ltd

native thyme
- Bush Tucker Supply Australia

paperbark
- Bush Tucker Supply Australia
- Gundabluey Bushfoods
- Robins Foods Pty Ltd
- some specialist gourmet food stores

quandongs
- Gundabluey Bushfoods
- Robins Foods Pty Ltd

riberries
- Bush Tucker Supply Australia
- Gundabluey Bushfoods

rosella flowers
- Bush Tucker Supply Australia
- Robins Foods Pty Ltd

rosella jam
- Robins Foods Pty Ltd
- Gundabluey Bushfoods (Robins Foods brand)
- Tasmanian Wild Foods at Pepper Berry Cafe

sweet lemon myrtle chilli sauce
- Australian Native Produce Industries Pty Ltd — Red Ochre Produce

venison
- Douglas Seafood and Game
- Australian Farm Venison
- Rossinis Fine Foods and Poultry
- produce markets
- some supermarkets
- specialist butchers
- some specialist gourmet food stores

wallaby
- Douglas Seafood and Game
- King Island Products
- produce markets
- some specialist gourmet food stores

warrigal spinach (greens)
- Robins Foods Pty Ltd

wattleseed
- Bush Tucker Supply Australia
- Gundabluey Bushfoods
- Robins Foods Pty Ltd

wattleseed linguini
- Australian Native Produce Industries Pty Ltd — Red Ochre Produce
- Gundabluey Bushfoods (Red Ochre brand)

wild boar
- Douglas Seafood and Game

witchetty grubs
- purchased in cans from gourmet delicatessens and some supermarkets

Suppliers addresses

We suggest that you phone before visiting any of the following outlets to ascertain that the product you require is in stock. Not all products are stocked continually, due to seasonal fluctuations in availability, so pre-checking is advisable.

Readers please note that telephone numbers Australia-wide are currently undergoing change to become 8-digit numbers. However, these changes are programmed to occur over a five year period so, although Melbourne, Sydney and Brisbane numbers will change within 1995 it will take another two to three years to upgrade all Australian numbers.

For Melbourne, Sydney and Brisbane numbers we have given the new telephone numbers in the following addresses as we believe they will be. If there is a problem please consult the information pages of your local telephone directory or directory enquiries.

A selection of produce markets:

Victoria
- Prahran Market
  163-185 Commercial Road
  South Yarra
  03) 9522 3302
  Open: Tuesday and Thursday dawn to 5pm; Friday dawn to 6pm; Saturday dawn to 1pm
- Queen Victoria Market
  cnr Victoria and Elizabeth Street
  Melbourne
  03) 9658 9600
  Open: Tuesday and Thursday 6am-2pm; Friday 6am-6pm; Saturday 6am-3pm; Sunday 9am-4pm (no meat or fish)
- South Melbourne Market
  Cnr Cecil and Coventry Streets
  South Melbourne
  03) 9695 8294
  Open: Wednesday 6am-2pm; Friday 6am-6pm; Saturday 6am-2pm; Sunday 8am-4pm

New South Wales
- Parklea Markets
  Cnr Surryholt Road and Old Windsor Road
  Parklea NSW 2155
  02) 9629 3311
  Open: Saturday and Sunday 8am-4.30pm
- Fish Markets Sydney
  Cnr Pyrmont Bridge Road and Bank Street
  Pyrmont NSW 2009
  02) 9660 1611
  Open: Seven days 7am-4pm

South Australia
- East End Markets
  266 Rundle Street (East)
  Adelaide SA 5000
  08) 232 5606
  Open: Friday, Saturday, Sunday 8am-6pm
- Central Market
  Gouger Street
  Adelaide SA 5000
  08) 203 7494
  Open: Tuesday and Thursday 7am-5.30pm, Friday 7am-9pm, Saturday 7am-1pm

Northern Territory
- Mindil Beach Market
  Mindil Beach
  Darwin NT 0800
  089) 81 3454
  Open: Thursday 5pm-10pm (end April to October) (includes over 60 food stalls from over 20 countries, including prepared and ready-to-eat bush tucker foods)
- Parap Markets
  Parap Shopping Centre
  Parap Road
  Parap NT 0820
  089) 88 1404
  Open: Saturday 8am-2pm

Western Australia
- Fremantle Markets
84 South Terrace
Fremantle
09) 335 2515
Open: Friday 9am-9pm; Saturday
9am-5pm; Sunday 10am-5pm, and
public holiday Mondays 10am-5pm

A selection of retail stores/
distributors:

- **Australian Farm Venison**
Dalry Park
Dalry Road
Healesville Vic. 3775
059) 62 3593

- **Australian Native Produce**
Industries Pty Ltd — Red
Ochre Produce
Head Office:
87 Harrison Road
Dudley Park SA 5008
08) 346 3337
Distributors:
South Australia
Gourmets Choice
Unit 4 Deacon Avenue
Richmond SA 5033
08) 234 2296

Coast and Country Food
Distributors
Box 641
Port Lincoln SA 5606
086) 82 2701

Victoria
Rosebuds
233 Williamsons Road
Templestowe Vic. 3106
03) 9846 4142

New South Wales
Gundabluey Bush Foods
8 Narraburra Close
Mount Colah NSW 2079
02) 9482 7305

Posh Foods Pty Ltd
Unit 9 Ashmore Estate
1a Coulson Street
Erskinville NSW 2043
02) 9550 6022

Queensland
The Australian Comestible
Company
36 Harlow Crescent
Noosa Parklands   Qld 4565
074) 74 0883

Gabrielle Cooney
30 Nolan Street
Whitfield Qld 4870
070) 32 0898

Red Ochre Grill
43 Shields Street
Cairns Qld 4870
070) 51 0100

Northern Territory
Parap Fine Foods
40 Parap Road
Parap NT 0820
089) 81 8597

Altitudes Bar & Eatery
1st floor, Darwin International
Airport
Sir Henry Wiggly Drive
Marrara NT 0810
089) 45 1120

Western Australia
PAT Foods
26 Munt Street
Bayswater WA 6053
09) 272 6522

Tasmania
Butterfields Tasmania
20 Letitia Street
North Hobart Tas 7000
002) 31 4214

Australian Capital Territory
Good Things
43 The Crescent
Queanbeyan NSW 2620
06) 297 4724

- **Blackwattle Deli**
Fish Markets Sydney
Cnr Pyrmont Bridge Road and
Bank Street
Pyrmont NSW 2009
02) 9660 1611
Open: see market hours
Stocks Gundabluey products

- **Bush Tucker Supply Australia**
Head Office:
482 Victoria Road
Gladesville NSW 2111
02) 9817 1060
Distributors and Agents:
Victoria
The Vital Ingredient
28 Eastern Road
South Melbourne Vic. 3205
03) 9696 3511

South Australia
Regency Food Services Pty Ltd
27 Taminga Street
Regency Park SA 5010
08) 268 8688

Western Australia
Mahogany Creek Distributors
Unit 1, Lot 140 Agett Road
Malega WA 6062
09) 249 2866

South-east Queensland
Bush Tucker Supply,
South-east Queensland
28 Kennedy Terrace
Paddington Qld 4064
07) 3368 3615
018 885 966

North Queensland
Garozzo Agencies Pty Ltd
38 Redden Street
Portsmith
Cairns Qld 4870
070) 35 3456

Northern Territory
Parap Fine Food
40 Parap Road
Darwin NT 0820
089) 81 8597

Australian Capital Territory
Poachers Pantry
Marakei Nanima Road
Hall ACT 2618
06) 230 2487

- **David Jones (Australia) Pty Ltd**
310 Bourke Street
Melbourne Vic. 3000
03) 9669 8200

- **David Jones (Australia) Pty Ltd**
Food Glorious Food
Market Street
Sydney NSW 2000
02) 9266 5544

- **Douglas Seafood and Game**
223 Rouse Street
Port Melbourne Vic. 3205
03) 9646 5081

- **Gundabluey Bushfoods**
8 Narraburra Close
Mount Colah NSW 2079
02) 9482 7305

- **Hermans Foods Pty Ltd**
59 Jersey Road
Bayswater Vic. 3153
03) 9720 3377

- **King Island Products**
351 Moorabool Street
Geelong Vic. 3220
052) 21 6399

- **Myer Melbourne**
314 Bourke Street and
295 Lonsdale Street
Melbourne Vic. 3000
03) 66 11111

- **Relishes Deli**
Shop 7/712 Prahran Market
Commercial Road
South Yarra Vic. 3141
03) 9826 1793
Open: see market hours
Stocks a selection of Red Ochre
Produce and Robins Bush Foods

- **Robins Foods Pty Ltd**
508 Lygon Street
Brunswick East Vic. 3057
03) 9386 1888

- **Rossinis Fine Foods and Poultry**
Shop K6 Chadstone Shopping
Centre
Princes Highway
Chadstone Vic. 3148
03) 9568 6215

- **Tasmanian Wild Foods at
Pepper Berry Cafe,**
91 George Street,
Launceston Tas 7250
003) 34 4589

- **Yuulong Lavender Estate**
Yendon Road
Mt Egerton Vic. 3345
053) 68 9453

155

Index